Unforgettable

STEVE THOMPSON

Unforgettable

Rugby, dementia and the fight of my life

BLINK
bringing you closer

First published in the UK by Blink Publishing
an imprint of Bonnier Books UK
Victoria House, Bloomsbury Square,
London WC1B 4DA

Owned by Bonnier Books
Sveavägen 56, Stockholm, Sweden

facebook.com/blinkpublishing
twitter.com/blinkpublishing

First published in hardback in 2022
This paperback edition published in 2023

Paperback ISBN: 978 1 78870 594 3
Hardback ISBN: 978 1 78870 590 5
Trade paperback ISBN: 978 1 78870 591 2
eBook ISBN: 978 1 78870 592 9
Audiobook ISBN: 978 1 78870 593 6

British Library Cataloguing-in-Publication Data:

A catalogue record for this book is available from the British Library.

Design by www.envydesign.co.uk

Printed and bound in Great Britain by Clays Ltd, Elcograf S.p.A.

3 5 7 9 10 8 6 4 2

Blink Publishing is an imprint of Bonnier Books UK
www.bonnierbooks.co.uk

To Steph, Seren, Slone, Saskia and Saxon,
for keeping me alive.

CONTENTS

Chapter 1

THE ANGEL AND
THE DEVIL

I've never googled dementia. I'm afraid of what it might tell me.

What I do know is the inside of my head is home to an angel and the devil. They argue constantly. In fact, their bickering wears me out. When the angel lifts me – 'You're allowed to feel good. It's OK to feel positive' – the devil immediately butts in – 'Forget it! You're coming back down. And quick.' There might not be anything in particular for me to feel bad about, but suddenly I feel terrible, like I'm about to be crushed beneath a gigantic black tyre rolling towards me.

I don't mind going through good times and bad times – that's just part of life – but this is different. I've been robbed of the ability to enjoy a good time, because the bad-time thoughts are overwhelming. I've always been a fighter, always found a way to sort stuff out, but this opponent not only isn't going away, its gathering force mirrors my declining ability to recognise its influence.

Dementia with probable chronic traumatic encephalopathy (CTE), a degenerative brain disease, stares me down from the opposite corner of the ring. The boxing comparison is apt – the only known cause of CTE is repeated blows to the head, hence the phrase 'punch-drunk'. Except while boxing matches are infrequent and last only a few rounds, my time being smashed extends to hundreds of ultra-competitive rugby matches plus endless brutal training sessions – thousands upon thousands of bangs, knocks, impacts and concussions, the vast majority of which were barely noticed by me, teammates, staff or opponents. 'Oh look,' a colleague would say as I lay on the deck, 'he's having one of his naps again.' Steve Thompson – he sleeps the sleep of the semi-conscious.

Every one of those collisions did its bit to form one of the ugly yellow pixels that, as I look at a scan of my brain, represents dead tissue. I carry that picture around on my phone. I show it to people like I show them pictures of my wife and children. 'Here we are on holiday last year. And if I just scroll along here's my CTE.' I've resisted the urge to have it as my screensaver. While it's there for all to see, nothing can ever be done about it. The damage is so deep that even Heineken can't reach it – God knows I've tried. In fact, the only way CTE can be diagnosed with 100 per cent absolute certainty is by post-mortem dissection. In the meantime, you'll have to take my and the experts' word for it. It's there. To be fair, the symptoms do add up. CTE affects emotions, steals memories, leaves the sufferer frustrated and irritable, and can lead to suicidal thoughts. I've never thought of myself as the perfect human specimen, but when it comes to CTE I most definitely am.

The result of all that battering to the brain – that CTE – is as stark as it is simple. I have dementia. It's described as being 'early stage', although already its effect is significant. I leave the car running in the street for hours on end. I go to fetch a beer from the fridge and find ten cans solidified in the freezer. I find myself stuck on the same book for months on end because I have to keep going back to the beginning.

The other day I was on at the dog for being a pain. 'Saxon! Saxon!' I was saying. It wouldn't even look at me. 'Saxon!' It was making me angry now. And then I looked at my three-year-old. He most definitely was looking at me – and he was terrified. What the hell was going on?

'You're calling the dog Saxon,' my wife Steph told me. 'His name's Stan. Saxon's your son.'

It was a proper *What was I thinking?* moment. People try to console me – 'Oh, I get my kids' names mixed up all the time.' And I think, *Yes, but not with the dog.*

And that's not the worst of it. I look at Steph, the woman I've shared everything with for ten years, including four children, and can't for the life of me remember her name. Let's just think about that for a second. How could not knowing your wife's name even be a thing? We all know our partner's name, right? It's second nature. There doesn't even have to be a link made in the brain. Name. Boom! There it is. Right there.

And yet in the past couple of years something unimaginable has happened, as bizarre as it is heartbreaking. Steph will be there in front of me, and I'll be staring at her – staring hard – and there'll be nothing. In my head I'll be thinking, *I know it! I know her name!* – like you might see someone momentarily stumped for the right answer on a quiz show. But the reality is this answer has gone. And unlike some stupid quiz show it matters. Knowing your wife's name really matters. In that moment, it's hard to think of anything that could possibly matter more – which in itself isn't a great help when you're desperately searching through the cluttered drawers of your mind, getting a fleeting glimpse of what you're after only for it to disappear again amongst the bric-a-brac, the tangle, the rubbish. It happens once and you think, *OK, that's just a one-off. A brain-freeze. It could happen to anyone.* I've seen it in the changing room. The captain looks at a bloke he's played alongside a hundred times and there it is – that moment where he can't propel his name to the front of his mind. Mildly embarrassing. Quite funny even for those watching. It happens. People get confused. But your partner's name? Really? Surely not ever. But I do it over and over again. One minute it's there, the next it's gone. Steph describes it as me turning into a complete blank. Like someone has switched me off at the mains. The only way to switch me on again is for her to say, quietly and firmly, 'I'm Steph.' At which point something unspoken, a recognition of what's happening, will pass between us and we'll carry on. Not that it makes it OK. Like any couple, when me and Steph married it was together forever. And suddenly, we have yet again been reminded, she finds herself with some bloke who can't even remember what she's called. She knows it's not me being mentally lazy, that I think so little of her that I genuinely can't instantly recall her name, but hard to imagine it's not hurtful. Somewhere, however deep, it must be. We're two sides of the same coin. Steph and Steve, Steve and Steph – not a hard one to remember. Like fish and chips, salt and vinegar – ruck and maul.

Other times we'll be having a conversation and I'll just stop mid-sentence. Totally gone. Like the drawbridge has been pulled up on my brain. Again, Steph has got used to it. She'll just give me a prompt – 'You were talking about this . . .' – but it's another nudge, another little reminder of what's happening, the riptide running silently beneath our feet, dragging us away from the shore. Dementia, it seems, can never be forgotten.

Guilt is the overriding emotion. I think it again and again – *This isn't what she signed up for. This isn't what I told her it was going to be.* And then, like a knee in the side of the head, I think, *What is her future going to be?* I don't mean that in some wishy-washy way; I mean, in the nuts and bolts of reality, what will it really be like for her looking after a husband with dementia? I look at her sometimes – *I can't believe what I've done to you. I won't be a husband, I'll be a patient. You won't be a wife, you'll be a nurse.*

Steph's the strongest person I know. So solid. So together. Her reaction to the diagnosis was simple – 'I'll care for you – of course I will. There's nothing more to say.' And I know she'll make it work. That's the way she is. She loves being a mum, looking after people. I couldn't love her more for that, but it doesn't stop me worrying. You don't get to play hooker for England if you're five foot two and weigh eight stone. I'm six foot three and eighteen stone. I'm OK for now but the time could well come when she'll need to move me, potentially carry me around, lift me off the toilet, put me in bed. What on earth will that be like?

I can't help feeling how far removed that nightmare will be from our original dream. Because we met quite late, we made a clear decision to have children quickly. The result of that is Seren (nine), Slone (seven), Saskia (five) and Saxon (three). The idea was that by the time they grew up, we'd still be young enough to have time to ourselves. We'd sacrifice some togetherness early on and get it back later in spades. After all, being fifty, sixty even, isn't like it was in the old days. When I was a kid, fifty-year-olds were proper old. They looked old, dressed old, acted old. Now all that's gone. Being older is a very different thing. People are incredibly active; their lifestyles are better. They live longer and stay young with it. We loved that idea – enjoying our time with the kids and then growing old together. Now that's been taken away, and that's where Steph does feel the injustice.

We were always going to enjoy those older years, and now, while physically we'll be together, there'll be the two of us sitting in front of the TV – ultimately, we'll be apart. Only one of us will know what the hell's going on.

That's without the effect on the kids. I love them so much but can't help but wonder how responsible it was to bring into the world children who are effectively, to one extent or another, going to have to look after me when they're older. I feel sick at what I'm going to leave them all to deal with. Steph will have me to care for, the kids to worry about, and then together they're all going to have to care for me.

There's a constant ebb and flow of contrasting emotions within me. One wave brings positivity – *OK, I've got something wrong with me, but we can understand it and work with it.* The next brings a tsunami of mental despair. *What am I going to put the kids through? How long do I have left before the clock stops and the bomb goes off?*

A couple of times I've been near tears. The other day Saskia came over and gave me a cuddle and a kiss on the forehead. 'What's that for?' I asked. 'You've got a poorly head,' she replied. I can only think she'd overheard a couple of mums talking to Steph about my diagnosis in the playground, but I still find it incredible that a four-year-old can zone in on a problem like that.

She's not the only one. The bedtime routine is I take the kids up for stories every night. When I've finished, they now all kiss my head before they go to sleep. They used to do the same to an elbow if I'd knocked it, or my hands if they'd swelled up through work. Feel your children's lips on your forehead in any circumstances and it's hard not to feel emotional. Now that emotion is times a thousand. When I shut their bedroom doors I just stand there on the landing trying to take it all in. It's lovely that they kiss my head, but at the same time it's so incredibly sad. I try to put on a brave face. It's one of them, isn't it? Do you show your true self and fall apart a little bit? Or do you hide things a little and just try to stay together for them? It's OK to say, 'It's good for the kids to see how you are.' But it's a fine line between that and scaring them. For a little kid a dad is their rock, and I'm not sure they will see me as a rock if I'm constantly falling apart. The time will come when they're a bit older to tell them properly. I don't want to frighten them now.

I might be a big bruiser of a bloke, but that doesn't mean I blunder through life without thinking. Truth is, at any given point, my brain is a swirling cauldron. What people see on the outside doesn't always match what's happening on the inside. The other day, for instance, when I was cuddling Seren, I could feel everything boiling up – frustration, anger, and that big overhanging question mark *Why?* mixed in with the intense love I felt for this beautiful little figure beside me. In that moment I felt myself breaking down. Luckily, Steph and the kids went out somewhere, and in their absence I managed to pull myself together. I don't ever want the children to see me cry. They shouldn't see their dad like that.

Other times, detachment is not so easy as hearing the front door slam. Some days not only am I living my experience but it feels like I'm watching myself live it, too. I look down on myself and think *Why am I here? I'm broken. It would be a lot easier for everyone if I just did myself in.* People brand those who take their own life as selfish – I have done exactly that myself in the past – but to do so totally ignores the headspace they're in. A lot of time they think they're being the absolute opposite of selfish. They believe they're doing it so that others around them can be spared the shrapnel of their problems. I'm no different. I start to think of the future in terms of the now. That the pain, the trauma, could be gone, for everyone, in the blink, the closing, of an eye. Short-term pain for long-term gain. *I could end this now. It's me who's the problem, so if I go then the problem goes with me. The kids will be better off without me. They'll escape from having to care for me. Yes, if I die, they'll be upset. But after a while they'll come to terms with what's happened and move on. It will be a lot less stress for everyone. I'll set them all free.*

At my lowest, Steph sees this bleak quandary in me. I got upset just the other day. 'I'm exhausted,' I told her. 'Just let me go. It's so hard to keep fighting, to have this constant good cop, bad cop thing going on in my head. And it can't ever really get any better.' She cradled my head like a baby. At times like that I'm as helpless as one.

The split-second threat that suicidal thoughts bring to me and my family isn't imagined – it's real. I was getting a train to London the other day, the first time I'd done so in a while. A lightning-fast inter-city came thundering towards the platform. It wasn't going to stop. The idea came from nowhere. *I could just jump in front of the engine. That's the way to do it. In a flash – gone.* I saw myself do it, as if I was being filmed from above. The express blasted through, engine and then carriages whizzing past me no more than two feet from my head. The sudden gust of air brought me back to reality. I started messaging Steph – *I'm on a mad downer.* And as ever she managed to calm me down. But in that moment the thought of ending it was so real I could touch it. *I could do this. I could actually do this.* In those lowest of times, Steph – amazing, understanding, incredible Steph – will always listen and talk me round.

Not long after, I was watching one of those emergency reality TV shows with Seren. There was a dad who was dying – his wife and their baby would be left without him. Seren broke down. 'I don't want anything to happen to you.' For a good while after she got really clingy. Sassy has been the same. I sit down and within seconds she's there. Same with Saxon and Slone. I'm so close to them all and I'm determined to push the dark thoughts away and keep them that way as long as I possibly can.

Sometimes, though, I wonder about those times when I feel a detachment from myself, from reality, as if I'm a viewer of my own life. Is that what it will be like when I'm further down the line? When I've reached a destination where there's no coming back. Will I be watching myself as others try to get through to me? Staring into my own blank eyes as others do the same? Trying to make sense of the nonsense I'm speaking. It's a question that can never have an answer. By then the time bomb will have stopped ticking – it will be too late.

That is why I am writing this book: to tell my story, to you, to my children – and to myself.

Chapter 2

FORGOTTEN

I was working away from home repairing a burst water main. Where once my work gear was rugby boots, shirt and shorts, now, flushing out water mains, it's all hi-vis vests and steel toe-capped shoes. Covid was at its peak and so I was in a bubble with another lad, Shaun. We worked and lived together for several weeks in Kendal, at the southern end of the Lake District. There was nowhere to go in the evening, no live sport on the telly, nothing. It felt like the world had forgotten how to live. To fill the void, ITV decided to show the entire 2003 Rugby World Cup. Shaun liked his rugby and suggested we give it a go. I'd never seen any of those games back. Why would I? I was in it. I was there. But throughout that July, Shaun and I watched England's journey to the final. Every night I'd cook us a bit of dinner and then we'd put the rugby on.

First up was our pool game against Georgia. As the minutes ticked by, something became clear to me – I didn't remember any of it. Shaun would ask me bits and pieces – 'What was he like? What happened there?' – and I could remember nothing. At one point I crossed the line to score. Great – except it was a bigger surprise to me than to my mate. I wasn't too worried. It was only a pool game, and a very routine one at that.

A few days later we were back in front of the TV for the second match, this time against one of the big boys – South Africa. Again, nothing. I might as well have been watching *Countdown* for all the physical and emotional connection I felt. It was like watching a stranger, not knowing who they were or what they might do next. The next encounter, versus Samoa, was exactly the same. Not a single spark of recollection. I was on the bench for our final group-stage match against Uruguay, but considering we won 111-13 you'd think there'd be at least one small nugget of recollection.

I'm sure Shaun must have thought I was mad. No wonder he tells everyone, 'He used to be my hero – then I met him.' But I kept putting the emptiness down to distance. I know to a lot of people that World Cup feels like yesterday, but it was in fact nearly twenty years ago. There's only so many games you can carry with you, and the early stages of a tournament aren't generally where the excitement and memories exist. The knockout games carry the lasting impressions, the high stakes. The first was the quarter-final against Wales. Steeped in rivalry, any clash between these two should be unforgettable, let alone a big World Cup encounter. But while I saw passion on the pitch, I felt none in my heart. The adrenaline that no doubt pumped through my veins that day had been replaced by sludge. The semi with France, a game with so much riding on it, was equally devoid of mental flashpoints. I might as well have been watching a rerun of an obscure Premier League football match. There was absolutely no connection, physical or emotional, as if I'd woken from a coma with no idea who I used to be. A spotlight was being shone on my life but I had no memory of being part of the show.

Maybe, though, there was one last chance. I began to wonder if, because the final became so all-consuming, so legendary, my mind had airbrushed those other games away. Why keep files you're never going to access? Why hang on to memories that have been made forgettable by what happened immediately afterwards? *Yes, perhaps that's it. It's not that there's something wrong with me. It's actually just my brain doing what anybody else's would do. I mean it's like a memory stick, isn't it? There's only so much space. Delete and replace – we all do it.*

And so there I am sat in front of the TV for the final. The teams run out on to the pitch, separated by the trophy. *Right,* I think, *don't remember that.* A massive cauldron of noise, 83,000 fans in the Telstra Stadium, half of it clad in white waving St George's Cross flags. People had headed out there in their thousands. *I do remember that. Or do I just know about it? I've seen it in pictures. I don't think that's me remembering something – it's just knowing it happened.*

Here's the national anthem. The boys are really going at it.

Lawrence Dallaglio is absolutely smashing it. It looks like his lungs are going to burst. And there's me. I look a bit nervous – on my toes, hopping about, big blow of the cheeks as 'God Save the Queen' finishes. *Was I nervous? I'm basically watching a stranger. How can anyone know what a stranger is feeling inside?*

Kick-off. Four minutes in and the Aussies score. Stephen Larkham sends a high kick straight into the hands of Lote Tuqiri. Jason Robinson's up against him on the try line but it's hardly a fair contest – Jason's seven inches shorter. *This is the best known, most remembered, game in the history of English rugby, and it might as well be live for all I can recall of what's going on.*

Two penalties from Jonny Wilkinson's golden boot put us in front. Concentrating for long periods isn't my thing any more and my mind starts to wander. There are questions I get asked all the time – and 'What was Jonny Wilkinson like?' is one of the more common. Bound to be – he became a national hero on the back of what he achieved at that tournament. Others include, 'What did Martin Johnson say in the dressing room before the final?' and 'What was Clive Woodward like as a bloke?' The honest answer to any question of this nature is always the same – I don't know. I feel an absolute fraud when people ask me these things and I say I can't remember. The look on their faces gives away what they're thinking – *He can't be bothered. He thinks he's too important to speak to the likes of me.* If it was the other way round, I'd be exactly the same – *Of course you can remember. What are you on about?* The last thing I ever want to do is come across as up my own arse. I find it absolutely mortifying that someone would think me so arrogant that I would brush them away; that I would willingly hurt their feelings. It reminds me of when I was a kid watching Northampton Town. Striker Trevor Morley was my big hero, his goals taking the Cobblers to the old Fourth Division title. One day I waited ages outside the stadium in the rain. Eventually he emerged. My big moment.

'Please can I have your autograph?'

'Fuck off,' he replied and got in his car. It broke my heart.

I've never forgotten that feeling. I never wanted to be like that as a player and, when people ask me to relive the excitement, the big moments, the fun we had and the scrapes we got into, I don't want anyone to think I haven't got time for them. I know I've lived their dreams and they just want to know a little bit about how that feels. I'm not being awkward. But there is nothing there. *Nothing there.* I simply don't know what to say and I'm embarrassed.

❖

My attention returns to the screen. Another Jonny pen and then Jason goes over in the corner for a try. I note how his celebration sees him punch the ball further than I could ever throw it in the lineout. The half-time whistle blows and we troop off, winning by 14 points to 5.

I often try to test my memory by thinking what the changing rooms in various stadiums were like. Again, ex-players are often asked about these things – who they sat next to, was there a team bath, that kind of thing – but I can't provide even the most basic of descriptions let alone reveal whose jockstrap was hanging off the light fitting, and the Telstra Stadium is no different. The only changing room I can recall is the shitty little one they used to have at Bath, a memory that unfortunately seems to be ingrained. Other than that, I wouldn't have the foggiest about any of them – Lansdowne Road, Murrayfield, the Millennium Stadium, Stade de France. Not even the changing room at Franklin's Gardens, Northampton, which was my home from home for a decade. I tell you, if I was stood on the pitch at Twickenham right now and someone asked me how to get to the changing rooms I genuinely wouldn't have a clue. I'd probably point them in the direction of the groundsman's shed.

The second half is under way. I see England dominate but the Aussies fight back to tie the scores at the final whistle. Before extra time I see our captain Martin Johnson giving us the gee-up. I assume he is anyway. I've no recollection of what he actually said.

England edge ahead again before Elton Flatley again ties the scores with a penalty. Even I know what happens next – ninety-nine minutes on the clock, there's a lineout. I throw the ball, find Lewis Moody, and the ball eventually ends up in the hands of Jonny. Lewis mentioned that throw to me recently. He told me it hit him straight in the nuts. 'I thought I'd aim at your brain,' I replied.

Jonny has barely half a second to line up the drop goal and kick between the posts before he's closed down. Occasionally,

I hear Ian Robertson's legendary commentary on BBC Radio 5 Live – 'He drops for World Cup glory! It's up – it's over! He's done it!' But there's no emotion in me, watching it, hearing it. Same as there isn't now. The referee blows and it's all over. I see a clip of me, Lewis and Jason Leonard laughing and celebrating. It's the sort of thing that should give me goosebumps. All I see is a fat lad, round head, big arse.

On the podium I spot myself stood between my fellow front-row forwards, Phil Vickery and Trevor Woodman. We're given our medals before Johnno lifts the World Cup. I see myself jumping about as the trophy is passed around. Normally, when you look back on a big occasion in your life, your heart rate increases, you feel excitement, the hairs on the back of your neck stand up. None of that happens. I don't expect it to. By now it's all become very obvious – that part of me, that version of me, is dead.

I held the World Cup and I don't remember it.

By all accounts, Prince Harry popped into the changing room afterwards. He might have spoken to me – I really have no idea. And that's the same with any of the celebrations that happened on the night, and those that came afterwards. I've seen photos of our arrival back at Heathrow, the crazy numbers who crammed into the arrivals hall at the horrendously anti-social hour of 4.30am to greet us, but the video in my head has been erased. The victory parade back in London is something else that people, understandably, want to talk to me about. They'll tell me where they were in the crowd. Or they'll just remember the incredible buzz of being part of a real moment in time. Something that had never happened before. Sporting history.

'Wow,' they say to me, thinking that whatever incredible emotions they experienced I must have felt 10,000 times more, 'that must have been amazing!' And why wouldn't they think that? All of us, a proper team of mates, who'd achieved the ultimate together, on an open-top bus winding through central London, waving, laughing, swigging champagne and beer, taking it in turns to lift the trophy in front of a sea of people. Maybe, like me – typical Thommo – putting it on my head (I've seen the pics). And yet all I can really do is nod or smile or look at them blankly. Again, I can't help thinking how disappointing that must be, or how rude people must think I am. But I can't remember being on that bus. It's the same with being shortlisted for World Player of the Year. I know it happened. It's there on Google. Beyond that, zilch.

Lewis recently sent me some photos of our time in Australia. I see us on the beach at Manly, in restaurants with various teammates sharing vast plates of ribs, enjoying a quiet morning in a coffee shop. It's not upsetting looking at old pictures. It can't be upsetting because that would mean there's some kind of emotional attachment to the image. But there isn't – there's nothing. *I know you*, I think as I look into my eyes, *but I don't remember being you.*

There's another photo in that little collection of post-World Cup euphoria. It's of the entire squad at Buckingham Palace for a picture with the Queen, a corgi trundling across in front of Her Majesty just at the moment the shutter clicks.

I'm in the back row for a change, grinning and, predictably enough, facing the wrong way. I saw it on Twitter not long ago and then looked at the shoes everyone is wearing. *So that's where I got them!* For ages I've had a favourite pair of shoes – soft brown leather – and been wondering where the hell they came from. Turns out, they're my official World Cup shoes. Well, I think I can call them that. I've had them mended so many times that they're like Trigger's old brush in *Only Fools and Horses* – only instead of seventeen new heads and fourteen new handles it's five new uppers and three new soles.

We'd be back at the Palace after being awarded the MBE in the New Year Honours, another momentous occasion which doubles as a blank page in my mental diary. I know bits and bobs about the day because Lewis has told me, which is something that can in itself be a source of confusion for people with early-onset dementia. I don't mean being spoken to by Lewis, although that is quite confusing, I mean the memories – owned and borrowed – that together form a congealed mulch in the brain. *Are these really my memories, or are they just things I've heard elsewhere?* The *BBC Sports Personality of the Year* show is a case in point. I know I went because I still have the plaque we were each given when we won Team of the Year. Beyond that, I recall absolutely nothing. I know, though, that if someone tells me about that night, my brain will try to take ownership of that memory. It might immediately vanish, it might linger for a while, or an echo of it might stay. If it does, I will eventually have no idea whether the memory is my own or if it comes from elsewhere. I'm so messed up I don't even know if I'm using my own brain.

My life post-World Cup was a whirlwind of functions, awards and events. But if there wasn't photographic evidence I totally wouldn't believe it, same as I wouldn't accept I'd spent that momentous evening in the Telstra Stadium in the first place. I was there – of course I was – but at the same time I was non-existent. If you have no memory of an occasion, the fact you were part of it is completely and utterly meaningless. How are you meant to bring it to life in your mind? How do you dig up a forgotten past and make it real? As far as I know, archaeologists don't search for long-lost brain cells. If I'm wrong on that one, please do give me a call.

For me, memory of the 2003 World Cup can only be rebuilt definitively by those I shared the experience with – the teammates and coaches who made that achievement possible.

It got me thinking. *I wonder if . . .*

Chapter 3

RECONSTRUCTION

I t's a strange thing asking people to rebuild a brain. It's all a bit *Six Million Dollar Man*, and that was Steve Austin, not Thompson. But I had a think about who was best placed to implant some reminders of a vanished glory. I thought about Lewis Moody, big daft Lewis – 'Mad Dog' by his own admission. The first England player to be sent off at Twickenham. A man who once gave Johnno a 'dig' in training and survived to tell the tale. A man as loyal to a cause as anyone I've ever known, who would run through brick walls – and massive Samoans – without a second thought. Lewis and I come from very different backgrounds – by his own admission he's a posh public schoolboy, a million miles from someone with an upbringing like mine – but, like me, he never prejudged anybody, and right from the start we just got on. He was very funny, not always intentionally, and had a habit of forgetting the pin number for his bank card at very convenient times.

Then there was Ben Cohen who, when I first encountered him as a teenager in Northampton, so generously christened me Shrek. Ben, of course, would never attract such a nickname. He's graced a thousand magazine covers, normally plastered in male grooming products and clad in a distressingly small pair of underpants. People would often say to me, 'How on earth are you friends with Ben?' But to me Ben's like a pair of trainers that are falling apart – you can't help putting them on now and then.

Lewis and Ben know me warts and all. Down the years, I've shared everything with them – the big stuff, the little stuff, and everything in between. Together we've travelled the world, got horrendously drunk, and won the World Cup. And now, all of a sudden, I've popped up, tapped them on the shoulder and said, 'Actually boys, I don't remember any of it.'

Paul Grayson (Grays), the long-serving Northampton fly-half, who also played in that 2003 campaign, was of a different generation to us three idiots. He'd seen something special in me from the start and had really taken me under his wing at Saints, for which I'll always be immensely grateful.

On the coaching side, Sir Clive Woodward was, of course, immense. It was his vision, his master plan, to get England playing a different way, one that not only would make us the best in the world but see us play some incredible rugby while travelling along that road. Clive's contribution, not just to rugby but to English sport, can never be overestimated.

I also had great respect for Andy Robinson (Robbo), Clive's number two. While Clive oversaw proceedings from a distance, Andy was much more hands-on, right at the centre of implementing the formula that would take us eventually to that big night in Sydney. Clive might have the odd word in the ear, whereas Robbo would just growl.

Specialist lineout coach Simon Hardy was the man who had the vast knowledge and even greater patience to take my nightmarish relationship with the lineout throw and turn it into something half-decent. Simon was relentless in his approach. He tracked me like that cop does Harrison Ford in *The Fugitive*. There were times I pulled back my curtains in the morning and fully expected his face to be pressed against the window.

Thankfully, all were happy to sit down and help put the jigsaw back together. What follows are the fruits of those conversations. Some memories are sweet; a few, particularly one or two of Ben and Lewis's, would really have been better left to rot on the tree! To all those who spoke on my behalf, who became my memory, I am forever grateful. I would like to refute here and now, however, Lewis's suggestion that I once dangled Rory McIlroy off a pub balcony.

Ben: In the lead-up to the World Cup I was rooming with Wally – he was Steve Walter when I first knew him [more on this later]. It was like being in with an animal – an animal who snores violently. Winning a World Cup is hard work. We were getting flogged in training and a bit of sleep would have been a great help. One night I'd had enough. 'For fuck's sake, Wall, shut the fuck up!'

He absolutely exploded. 'That's it!' he spluttered. 'That is fucking it!' He was having a right go at me, calling me every name under the sun, as if I was the one causing the problem. 'I've had enough,' he said, 'I'm going.'

He got up, pulled this huge queen-sized mattress off his bed and dragged it into the bathroom. The mattress was so big and the bathroom so small that he had to fold it in half like a piece of bread, with him the hot dog in the middle.

'Right,' he said, 'fuck off! I'm going to sleep.'

'Night, Wall.'

I gave it a couple of minutes and knocked – 'Wall,' I said, 'I need to use the toilet.' He went off his absolute rocker. I thought about the consequences of pushing the situation. 'It's OK, mate,' I told him. 'I'll do it in a bottle.'

Wally and I have a long history of room-sharing disputes. In a twin room, most hotels would stick a double and a single. We'd race each other to the corridor before a violent battle to be first through the door. On one occasion, I forced my way in before him and jumped on the double bed only for the legs to give way. Immediately, I leapt across on to the single – 'Yours is the double, Wall!' He had to sleep on a 45-degree angle. And that's exactly what he did. Wall, the great snorer, would sleep through anything.

Lewis: I would share with Thommo a lot. He had a long-running problem with psoriasis – and two possible solutions.

One was to let the skin see the sun. The other was to apply an all-over body cream and let it air-dry. When I was sharing with Thommo he always seemed to choose the second option. After a while I could guarantee one thing – whenever I came back to the room with my wife or agent, also a woman, we'd be confronted by a stark-bollock naked Thommo casually wandering round the room slowly drying off.

Steve: *To be fair, I did used to spend my time doing other things.*

Lewis: Thommo had an air rifle. We'd spend a lot of time at the England training HQ at Pennyhill Park, in Bagshot, not too far from Twickenham. It was a converted old manor house, big place, backing on to a forest, and surrounded by acres of grounds. We had a lot of downtime and the lads were always finding ways to entertain themselves. PlayStations and reading were popular. Thommo brought along a gun. Our entertainment became rifle shooting. At first it was a cardboard fox on the window ledge. That progressed to setting up cans out the back of our window. We used to hide the rifle under the bed, away from the cleaner, but word must have got round because one day a staff member approached Thommo. We feared the worst, but actually he mentioned there was a bit of a pigeon problem and wondered if Thommo could possibly help. From that point on, whenever he wasn't in training, Thommo would wander round the hotel with his rifle and perch himself in various positions like an *Assassin's Creed* sniper, picking off pigeons left, right and centre. God knows what people thought was going on.

Steve: *This is why I wanted people other than Ben and Lewis to contribute their memories – so there'd be something in this chapter other than what an idiot I was. I mean, surely I was an OK player as well?*

Grays [Paul Grayson]: When you're an older player you occasionally hear names of local kids who are doing good things. At Northampton, Ben and Steve's names came up as boys who had some potential – as well as some seriously rough edges. When I first met Wally, he was a very, very capable tearaway. Sometimes you see potential and think, *Crikey, if they can just get it right, there's no limit to where they can go as a player.* When Steve began to progress to hooker, I wrote an article for the *Northampton Chronicle & Echo* basically saying that Steve Thompson could be the best player in the world in his position. He absolutely had the lot, freakishly so.

Steve: *According to Grays, things really started to happen for me when England took me on their tour of North America in 2001.*

Grays: We'd gone to Los Angeles to play America A at UCLA, a classic fly-in-fly-out tour game. Steve had a knee injury but came on as sub in the back row with about fifteen minutes to go, the first time Clive Woodward had seen him properly up close – it was a university so we were just standing on the side of the field. In those fifteen minutes Wally absolutely tore it to shreds. He beat people, won physical collisions, and really looked the part. I can remember it clear as crystal. That was the moment the light bulb clicked with Clive. You could see him thinking, *I've found something here.* That was the game that sealed Wally's future. If he could learn to throw properly he was going to be immense.

Sir Clive: To a man, the team that won in 2003 was exceptional – I was blessed with some amazing players across the field – but the one position I felt we weren't world class in was hooker. I searched for the final part of the jigsaw. From nowhere came Steve. Fast, courageous, skilful. I knew then we had the team to win the World Cup.

Steve came to America with us as a back-row forward, more to be with the squad than anything. He was a big tough guy and I liked him straight away. I clearly remember saying to him, 'The problem is, Steve, you're up against Lawrence Dallaglio, Richard Hill and Neil Back.' Lewis Moody was in that mix as well. It was then that I asked him, 'Have you ever thought about playing in the front row?'

Grays: I'd gone on that tour as the kicking coach. England's best players were away with the Lions. I told Trevor Woodman, Steve Thompson and Phil Vickery, 'You three will be the front row for England in the World Cup.'

Clive: Everyone thought Jason Leonard and Graham Rowntree would start the World Cup at one and three. They were good players, good scrummagers, but in the back of my head I knew that if we wanted to do something more we had to change the whole vision of the front row. So many hookers and props saw the position as scrums and lineouts. That to me was just the start. I needed the team to go to a new level. Yes, a front-row player has to scrummage, but that's just the basics; that's what gets them in the team. When it came to Woodman, Thompson and Vickery, I could really talk to all three of them. I told them I wanted them to do far more than scrummage: 'We won't win the World Cup by just being great at scrummages. We'll lose it if we're not great at scrummages, but we certainly won't win it.

'If a front rower wants to win a World Cup,' I told them, 'they've got to run round the pitch, tackle, pass. They've got to play like back rowers.'

Robbo [Andy Robinson]: The days of the old hooker, who was maybe a little bit podgy, were disappearing. Thommo's speed meant that he could play in the wider channels, and that's what we saw about him playing in the front row. His athleticism and power offered the England team so much.

Lewis: We were used to players like Brian Moore and Richard Cockerill, small blokes, as hookers. They were seen to fit easier into that middle part of the front row. Thommo was the opposite. He was the size of a back rower and significantly heavier. When we first met, he was actually a number six and I was a number eight. He didn't even get to play. But as a hooker, he was a pioneer. He came into his own at scrum time in terms of bossing it around. I loved how much he controlled it, even when he first came into the squad.

Ben: He had everything – great footwork, he could link, run over people. He was also someone who, if necessary, could be a bit old school, get down and dirty, which every great team needs. It was like someone had made the perfect hooker.

Clive: Phil Larder, our defence coach, loved Steve, because he could tackle, he could hit, he could do everything like a back rower. In my mind I began to see that front row of Vickery, Thompson, Woodman. Vickery and Woodman weren't massive – in fact, whereas normally hookers are smaller than props, Steve was bigger than both – but, similar to Steve, they were very athletic. I asked our specialist scrummaging coach, Phil Keith-Roach, about Steve. 'What do you think? Can we do this?' As a player, I'd never thrown a ball at a lineout or been in the scrum – it was a dangerous place I'd never wanted to go! – and so if I wanted to make Steve the best hooker in the world, I needed that expertise. After a couple of sessions with Steve, Phil's answer was clear: 'If he wants to do it, he can do it.' Suddenly we had this kid, Thompson. The rest is history.

Steve: *I was lucky that I came into the England squad when I did. Eighteen months later and I'd never have enjoyed that glory. Yes, you need ability, but you also need so much luck to go with it.*

Ben: Wally was really up against it when he came into that World Cup-chasing team, one of the last to do so. He epitomised the sheer application needed to reach that level.

Clive: He had to work hard. He had all the back-row skills. No doubt about it, he was a back-row forward. It was a big shift for him, like asking Lawrence Dallaglio if he wanted to play hooker. In Lawrence's case, he'd have just looked at me and said, 'You've got to be joking!' Steve said, 'Yes, I want to do it.' He knew this was a special group of players with the potential to really do something and saw there was a hole at hooker. He knew that if he could get the lineout right he'd be in the team.

Steve: *Easier said than done. When I started out as hooker I had zero confidence in my ability to throw the ball at a lineout. At Saints, if we had the ball in our 22 and kicked it long I'd be desperate for the opposition to run with it rather than send a long kick back. If they did take the aerial route, I'd feel a shiver go down my spine. If that kick goes into touch, I'm going to have to throw it. Don't go out! Don't go out! And, of course, out it would go. That might sound stupid but it wasn't like my move to hooker, for club or country, had come over time. It was virtually an overnight conversion and so I didn't have anything remotely resembling a grooved throwing* *technique. I'd have been lucky to hit a barn door. And a hooker who can't throw is like a goalkeeper who can't save. That was how I first met Simon Hardy.*

Clive: I literally told Simon, 'Go and live with Thompson – spend every hour you can with him.' He's got to be world class at throwing-in. Everything else he can do.

Simon [Hardy]: The first time I went to Steve's house I asked for a coffee. He made me a Nescafé. 'I'm not coming in if you're serving me that,' I told him. 'I haven't driven halfway up the M1 to drink Nescafé!' Lesson learned; within twenty-four hours he'd got a machine. And then that was it, we'd be out on the driveway throwing.

Steve: *Simon was the person who turned me into a respectable lineout thrower. Any hooker on England's radar, Simon worked with them. As a player, you get lucky with the coaches that come into your life. I was never luckier than with Simon – he just got me. Good job, really. I can remember enough about my character at that stage to know that if me and Simon hadn't got on, I wouldn't have cooperated with him. I'd have been an arsehole, totally not interested. Rather than just swallow it up, I'd have cut my nose off to spite my face. Having said that, the Nescafé incident did almost wreck everything. I might as well have served him a cup of boiled rabbit shit.*

Robbo: So long as he saw the sense in it, Steve was always able to take feedback. While he didn't sometimes like what he heard, he was able to use it in the right way to enhance his performance. Because of that he was able to reach the peak – to get everything out of his career.

Steve: *Robbo could be a pretty tough taskmaster but he was a brilliant coach, mainly because he himself, like Simon, was always willing to learn. Rather than a one-size-fits-all approach, he'd look at different players, take the best bits, and then work with them to make them even better. The best coaches are always adaptable. Just telling someone, 'Right, this is the England way,' and expecting them to get on with it is counterproductive. That just shows you don't understand how people think and work. A good teacher is way more subtle than that. That's not to say he wouldn't challenge a player. If he felt it was needed, he'd get in your face. Again, that was good for me. It was exactly what I needed. I was at an age, early twenties, where I was perfectly capable of being a dick at times.*

Robbo: I could question Steve, I could push him, but I knew he always had that close support with Simon. For a player, when you've got coaches challenging you, maybe criticising you, to have that one person there is massive. That relationship was huge. You need a mentor to support you. That's where Simon was brilliant – all the unseen work he did with Steve was phenomenal.

Simon: When you work one-on-one with players, you get to know them. You get under their skin and see the real them. Steve was very much into the mastery of the skill, whereas a lot of his other game was based on ego. He worked hard on his throw because it wasn't natural, but he had a real ego when he scrummaged. I'd seen him at club level in training. There was a lot more banter with his scrummaging – he'd be putting people through the mill. Players are different. Jonny Wilkinson was all about mastery. Chris Ashton was all about ego. When it came to throwing, Steve thrived on that mastery. He was pragmatic. He wasn't worried about practice sessions being exciting, he just wanted success. He just wanted to be told straight what he needed to do.

Steve: *Simon taught me where my elbows and hands should be. He taught me about the importance of timing and hitting my targets.*

Simon: The normal person in the street might think a hooker picks up a rugby ball, stands there, and chucks it down the line, but there's so many technical elements involved – posture, balance, angles, distance, handling technique. Some of the issues I identified were a hangover from Steve's childhood days as a basketball player. The two disciplines require a very different wrist position and when he got tired on a rugby pitch it wasn't uncommon for him to sink back into those old ways. Instead of targeting the ball, he'd loop it. He also had a slight left shoulder injury which meant his left elbow came out wide. At least his hands were the right size. Hookers with hands that are too big or too small struggle with the ball. The perfect hooker is a bit of a Frankenstein's monster. What might be an attribute in the front row, such as big solid shoulders and stocky legs, isn't necessarily compatible with what's needed as a thrower. You have to stick various bits together, give them a tweak and hope that they work. I never pretended I was going to make him the best thrower of a rugby ball the world had ever seen, but I was confident I could get him to the point where he could throw efficiently. I'd seen enough early on to know he wasn't a natural thrower but felt that together we could build a robust technique.

Robbo: It shows a determination on Steve's part to make that transition to hooker work as well as it did. To play in the front row takes something, it really does, and the way he went about it was tremendous. As soon as Steve became able to throw and scrummage, and improved his technique defensively, he became the number-one player for us.

Grays: I can't ever remember there being a question of anybody else even getting within a whisker of that Number 2 shirt.

Lewis: All of a sudden, he was flying. He went very quickly from not being involved to starting and, once he was in, there was no getting him out. He was such a revelation. He was massive, strong, quick, had great handling skills, and now he could throw as well.

Ben: It makes such a massive difference when you've got a front row that is so agile and can play. In the run-up to that World Cup, Wally, Vickery and Woodman created a front row which was untouchable. They were the definition of the new breed of front rowers, amazing to play behind because you knew you were going to get ball on the front foot.

Clive: The English forward pack used to play slowly. I had a very clear view of how the game should be played if you want to win at the top level. We spent a lot of time studying the All Blacks. In the end, I just said it: 'The only way to beat the All Blacks is to outplay the All Blacks – you have to play quicker than them.' Quick, quick, quick. It wasn't headless chicken stuff. It was ball in the scrum – in, out, play. Ball in the lineout – in, out, play. Tap and go. Speed of thought. I wasn't doing that for philosophical reasons. I was doing it because, play quickly, with everybody on fire, and we had a better chance of winning against the top teams. If you want to have a kicking festival against Scotland or Wales, fine. But if you want to beat the All Blacks, South Africa, Australia, away from home, you've got to find a different way. For me we had to play in such an un-English way that no one would recognise us. And that's what we did. We had a forward pack that was unrecognisable – literally. In Thompson, Woodman and Vickery, we had three back rowers playing in the front row. My job was to make every individual buy into that idea – Dallaglio, Johnson, Steve, all of them. 'I don't want to be faffing around – we're going to be fitter than the other team and we're going to run them off the pitch.' The speed of that team was unbelievable, and that was one of the key reasons for our success, not just in the World Cup but over a four-year period during which we were almost unbeatable. Playing this way worked. We were the most successful sporting team England had ever had, not just in rugby – anything. Steve was key in making that happen. Absolutely. I make no bones about it.

Robbo: The beauty of that side was everybody had a role, everybody understood that role, and everybody knew how to deliver that role under pressure. Everything didn't go right on the day, but the team's focus was always on what they could control and what happens next as opposed to dwelling on what had just happened. It was a side that was able to cope with a setback, just as it had five months earlier when going down to thirteen men against New Zealand at Wellington – England's first victory over the All Blacks on New Zealand soil for thirty years. The fact we'd also beaten Australia in Australia earlier that year meant that, while the guys understood the All Blacks were a threat, they knew also they could withstand anything they threw at us. That showed the confidence they had in each other, and Steve was a big part of that.

Steve: *That All Blacks game at Wellington is one which should be as memorable as any I've played in. I actually heard it mentioned on the radio the other day. Again, for all the connection I felt, I might as well not have been there.*

Ben: The good thing about that team was the fact that, because we'd already played and won a lot of big games, we knew we had everything. While, understandably, people will always want to talk about the World Cup final, truth is there were games leading up to that match that were a lot more character-building, had a lot more to them. We were coming off our peak when we won the tournament, but we still had everything in our armoury. We could still perform and deliver.

Robbo: Everyone understood what they had to do for that World Cup final. Steve, like the whole team, did all the preparation. I've always believed that if you've worked hard, you've made the improvements, then you can't do any more. Get out there and perform. They knew they were ready, and it showed when the scrum suddenly started to get penalised by the referee for what we considered the wrong calls. We were still able to absorb that situation and deal with it, testament not only to the training the players had put in but to the relationships they'd created with each other. As a captain, Martin Johnson was a great person to follow but he allowed other people to make decisions. Steve would do just that if he felt it was appropriate. He was very focused on performance and would come up with good opinions. I liked that when things became difficult he would express how he felt. Steve was an emotional lad who'd been through a lot in life. What he'd learned through those experiences was the ability to express himself at the right time.

Ben: Wally had a lot of leadership characteristics which I and others liked. He'd get you up for a game.

Clive: In a team you tend to have players who never shut up. Then there's another group who sit there and take it all in – when they speak everyone listens. Steve was more of the latter – really bright, a great team player, a huge contributor, and if he felt there was something he needed to say he'd say it. Nowadays in coaching, we call it 'psychological safety'. You create a team environment where if someone thinks something's not right, they can stand up and say it, whether or not it might upset a teammate, coach or whoever. Psychological safety means you can trust players to be honest. I wanted that team to be challenging, emotionally intelligent enough to put forward views, and feel safe that they could do so. Steve was a great example of that. I knew that if anything wasn't stacking up, he would tell me. Team meetings were lively at times, to put it mildly, but that was because we wanted to win. I encouraged that environment and encouraged Steve to speak up because he was so good at it.

Lewis: Thommo wouldn't just talk unnecessarily. When he spoke he did so with purpose and strength. When you look at the players in that World Cup squad, to be a strong voice and character in that group wasn't easy. But he wouldn't hold back. If a senior player had a pop at him, he'd be having a pop back straight away. It showed them he was there and he meant business. He was respectful but strong-willed with it – plus he was massive, obviously!

Robbo: Thommo's openness helped us as coaches understand how to channel his character into his performances.

Ben: The best competitors are strong characters. When England got to that 2003 World Cup final, that's exactly what we had, and Wally was right up there with the strongest of them, off the pitch and on it.

Grays: He was a very likeable character, good fun to be around, with some exceptional physical and mental traits. Young and loose, but with a charm about him. I enjoyed our team nights out. He'd always be up to something but it was generally quite funny and harmless. He had a mischievous side but also knew how to read a situation, and people. He had a good sense of place – 'Right, where am I in the pecking order?' I never found him one of those younger guys who you'd be thinking, *He needs to wind his neck in.* He wasn't banging the drum or speaking at every break in play. He wasn't putting himself up there with Dallaglio, Johnson, Matt Dawson, as the England lynchpins.

Steve: *From what I remember, I got on with everyone in that 2003 England World Cup set-up. Lewis tells me I fitted in really well – maybe not that easy when you're the last one into the inner sanctum. But then again, I've always taken people for the way they are. Don't* *judge a book by its cover and all that. I'll talk to a homeless person on the street the same as I'll talk to a top CEO. Rugby helped me massively with that. It gave me the ability to speak to anyone. I love it when people meet me and say, 'You're different to how I thought you'd be – I thought you'd be a bit up your own arse,' because hopefully that means I'm entirely the opposite.*

Lewis: When I first came across Steve at England Under-21 level, he was totally different to anyone I'd ever met. I'd come from a public-school background so was fairly blinkered, and here was this straight-talking, blunt, rough around the edges young man. But that was just first impressions. Once I really started to get to know him, learned his story and saw how competitive he was, same as me, as well as his key characteristics of protectiveness and loyalty, I could see how similar we were. Of course, we both liked a laugh, messing about, which appealed to me as well. Thommo was a very impulsive character – things would change at the drop of a hat – which made him good fun to be around. But we were both very, very good at leading each other astray.

Steve: *It was the same with me and Ben – like chalk and cheese but somehow we got on. Because we'd known each other right from the early days, we just never held back – not so much banter as abuse. People took the piss, that's how the game was. It was no-holds-barred humour that somehow held everyone together. Of course, underneath, that person would know you'd got their back all the way.*

Ben: In rugby, you have to have incredible honesty or you're going to fall at the first hurdle. Wally will always say it how it is, and that's how I see myself. When you spend pretty much five, six years together, literally in each other's pockets, you're so way past normality that you talk in a different way. We were all mates in that World Cup team. I liked the fact that Wally and I could talk very frankly and have fun together.

Robbo: Steve was a popular guy amongst the squad. He was cheeky and liked the banter. But there was much more to him beneath the surface. He was very giving. He was interested in you as a person and was very engaging.

Simon: Steve was lively round the camp, but he was humble more than arrogant.

Lewis: One of the things I always admired about Thommo was that, while it took me ages to really feel comfortable in the England environment, he seemed to fit in straight away. It wasn't just Ben and me – the team took to him very quickly as well. Thing is, get to know Thommo and you find there's actually a quieter, more sensitive guy underneath. He's very kind and always looks out for his mates; a good example was during that World Cup campaign. We'd had a big night out, given carte blanche to enjoy ourselves so long as we were at the team meeting at nine the next morning. As the night wore on, a few of the other lads trickled back to the hotel but me and Thommo pushed on. No two ways about it, by the end of the night we were well drunk. At one point I flicked Thommo in the plums (I should mention here that Steve had something of a trigger temper) and he reacted by uppercutting me in mine, at which point I collapsed to the floor, partially laughing, partially in agony. Not wanting to let it go, I nudged Thommo into a door. Either I nudged him too hard or he was more drunk than I thought, because he ended up headbutting the door frame, splitting his eyebrow open, blood everywhere. I stood there holding an ice cube on his eye for the rest of the night. The reason this story comes under the heading of 'kindness' is that I woke up the next morning lying on my bed still in my clothes. My head was literally banging, or so I thought. It was actually Thommo thundering on the door. Clive was an absolute militant for 'Lombardi time' – the principle whereby if you're not early for a meeting then you're late. And if you were late, it was a real black mark against you. Thommo had got to the meeting early, seen that I wasn't there, and come looking for me. You could say he saved my World Cup. Had I not made it on time it would have been frowned upon massively. That was very decent of him all things considered.

Steve: *If I got on with someone, that was all there was to it. I hate it when one minute you hear someone slagging a person off behind their back and the next they're all over them in the flesh. I can't get my head round that. If I like someone, I like them, and* *that's that. It's just an honest approach, same as if we had a day off I'd maybe just chill out on my own for a few hours at the team hotel rather than feel I had to be with other people.*

I liked the variety of characters around the squad. Jason Robinson was a case in point. Because he'd found religion, I do remember having different sorts of conversations with him than I might some of the other players. I enjoyed that change of scene. In any team I played in I never liked it when players got so close that it was almost like they wouldn't let others in. I'd see it sometimes with the lads who played cards. One minute they'd all be loving each other and then suddenly one of them would be dropped from the group. Before his seat was even cold, another player would slot in and they'd be best mates with him instead.

Lewis: He always seemed really grounded. Clearly there were other Northampton players in the group, Matt Dawson and Grays, for example, and maybe that helped. His time growing up with the Saints, alongside guys like legendary England lock Tim Rodber, whom he absolutely idolised, meant he also had a real focus and determination. He credited Rodders for a huge amount of his success in rugby.

Steve: *As well as Rodders, Northampton's Scottish international prop Mattie Stewart was another who kept me firmly in the real world. When I first got in the England squad, I was driving a sponsored Mercedes and being paid to wear Nike kit. Now that, in anybody's books, is amazing. I'd come back from England duty to our shared digs and say to Mattie, 'Come on! Get the kettle on!'*

and he'd be like, 'Oh, changed have you? Giving it the big one because you've played for England?'

Ben: I will say Wally wasn't always as confident as he looked. His first England game, the year before the World Cup, was against Scotland at Murrayfield. He was really nervous. We were sitting in our room and he said to me, 'Why am I here? How am I playing for England?' The national team was so strong at that point, I think we both thought we were blagging it.

Steve: *Ben definitely deserved to be in that England side, but it would make me laugh how luck always seemed to be in his corner. We once pulled over at the side of the road for a slash and right there on the floor next to him was a two-pound coin. On a windy day, you can bet I'd be brushing leaves off my face and he'd have a tenner stuck to his forehead.*

One very bizarre thing I've never forgotten about my England debut is I could have been wearing the Scotland jersey that day. We'd played Edinburgh at Northampton and my teammate, the Scot Richard Metcalfe, notable for being seven feet tall, invited me round to his house the next morning for coffee. I thought it was a bit odd – me and Richard weren't particularly close – but went along anyway. I walked in and there was Frank Hadden, the Edinburgh coach. I wondered if Ian McGeechan, the recently departed director of rugby at Northampton, and now in the same position with the Scotland national team, had given Hadden a nudge. After all, if Edinburgh signed me, and I lived up there for a few years, I'd be eligible through residency to play for Scotland.

'I'm sorry,' I said, 'I'm English.' I really don't think it would have worked. The Scots just don't seem to like me. I was once blank refused a sausage sandwich in a café north of the border. I had to get a Scottish mate to go up and get it for me.

Ian McGeechan: The meeting with Frank Hadden was nothing to do with me! Actually, as it worked out, I was the Scotland coach in that game when Steve made his debut. I always took a lot of pride in seeing where players I'd worked with took themselves, so from a personal point of view I was hugely delighted to see him on the field that day and to see what he achieved with England.

Clive: He soon became ever-present. That was good for him but bad for us because the risk was if he got injured there'd be a big gap. Everyone else in that side was replaceable, even Jonny Wilkinson. I'm totally confident that we'd have still won that World Cup if Paul Grayson had started at ten because he was that good at goal-kicking. But if Steve wasn't there, it would have been a real blow. In most positions you have back-up that's pretty close to what you're replacing. The hooker on the bench was Dorian West, a great player, but a more traditional worker. Once Steve got in the team, he was above anybody else. I wouldn't have swapped him for anybody. Nobody. No one in South Africa, New Zealand, anywhere.

Robbo: England as a whole had become an adaptable team, capable of playing in many different ways. Australia scored a try early in the final. When we came back with a try of our own from Jason Robinson, the offloading skills of Lawrence Dallaglio and the support skills of the other players showed how good we were.

Lewis: It was a tight game. I came on in extra time. I wasn't nervous, because I'd achieved my overriding priority to get to a cinema the night before. Going to a movie before every England game was my number-one superstition, a distraction which soon became a routine. The only time I hadn't done it was a few months earlier in Marseilles when we'd lost for the only time in our previous twenty-two games. Imagine my utter horror, therefore, when Thommo and I arrived for the final screening of the racehorse drama *Seabiscuit* at 9.30pm only to discover the projectionist packing his gear away. No one else had turned up, he explained. There was only one thing to do – pay the bloke to put it on for us. Kindly, he agreed. I say 'kindly', but actually Thommo had to pay him a hundred quid for the privilege – and then he still charged us for our tickets! Steve paid for those as well. Out of nowhere I'd forgotten my PIN number.

Steve: *No wonder I aimed at his balls in that final lineout. Although hitting a six-foot three-inch target – that's Lewis not his balls – wouldn't have been as simple without mental preparation.*

Ben: The problem with someone who lineout throws is their confidence can easily take a whack. Steve would talk about it, and I'd say, 'Mate, just chill. We're all like that. We all have issues with confidence and trying to recreate your best ball. It's part of being a professional athlete.'

Simon: I tried to build him up mentally. I identified, for instance, that he was nervous walking to the touchline for a lineout. 'If you're nervous, and you look nervous,' I asked him, 'how do you think the lineout is going to feel? You've got to look the part. You've got to be a little more brash. Your body language has got to be good.'

Steve: *I have a vague memory of seeing a sports psychologist – they were coming in more and more during my career. One concluded that I was better on autopilot than over-analysing what I was doing. This was passed on to Robbo. 'So, hang on,' he said. 'We've spent all this money on a sports psychologist and all he's come up with is, "If Thommo thinks about something, he's had it?"'*

Simon: It was important he didn't waste mental energy and accept that with any throw there was a whole series of things out of his control. Someone in the lineout could make the wrong call, somebody else might mistime their jump, or a referee might make a wrong judgement. I wanted him mentally to boil the whole process down to just throwing the ball, to always be positive. Part of that was developing a trigger phrase he could access as he stepped up to the touchline and threw. The idea was it would deter him from thinking, *Right, got to get the knees in, hips up, chest up*. Overthinking is a danger in sport. Look at golfers who fluff a simple putt to win a championship. They will have sunk that putt a thousand times, so what suddenly is the problem? Real pressure? Or imaginary pressure? We came up with not so much a phrase as a noise – 'PPPSSSS!' which matched the tempo of his throw. Time and again I would ask him what he was thinking as he approached the touchline, and time and again he'd forget what I meant and give me some stupid reply.

'What the hell are you doing?' I'd shout. 'It's really simple. There's only one answer!'

It was all about keeping him mentally oiled. I made a video reel of Steve's best throws and put his favourite music to it. That way, whenever he heard that piece of music he'd automatically think of his best throw.

Robbo: Steve recognised the importance of the lineout and did everything he could to make himself as good as he could possibly be. We'd lost to Ireland in 2001 and been ripped apart at the lineout. Everybody blames the hooker when the lineout doesn't go right but sometimes it's your jumping combinations, what jumpers you have, and the way that the opposition has studied your set-up. It was a time when the competitiveness of the lineout was huge. We only hung on to beat New Zealand at Twickenham in 2002 because Ben Kay stole an injury-time lineout on our line, which ultimately denied New Zealand victory.

Simon: Before a game I'd create a lineout menu. A lot of it was based around visualisation. I'd talk about the opposition, the movements, the shapes – prepare Steve for what he was likely to see. In the World Cup we played a couple of pool games at Perth, an oval Aussie Rules ground with a rectangular pitch in the middle. That arrangement makes visualisation much harder for a player because spatially it doesn't conform to anywhere else they've played. The kickers would always practise in a stadium at a time comparable to the match day to get an idea of conditions, and Steve and I would go throwing too. We'd go all the way round the pitch to get used to different visualisations. We'd also look at wind conditions and factors such as how they might be affected by gaps in stands.

Clive: Jonny's drop goal started with Steve throwing the ball in. He was under huge pressure. He doesn't throw the ball in straight to Lewis at the back of the lineout and we don't win the World Cup.

Simon: The lineouts for both teams didn't quite go to plan. They won a lot of ours; we won a lot of theirs. Partly that's a freak of the game, but also, towards the end of a tournament, there's a lot of analysis going on. I spent hours going through all their lineouts and calls and I'm guessing they did the same. They would have picked up certain bits and pieces about us just as we had about them. That puts you under pressure. In that game we also had a relatively small back row by international standards – competent jumpers, but you wouldn't call them towering. The French, for example, tended to have three six-foot-six boys.

Steve: *From the outside I can see that lineout would look like a big pressure situation, but I don't ever remember being nervous during any England game. I'd go into schools to talk to kids as part of Saints' community programme. I found that much more nerve-racking than playing in front of 80,000 people. Kids don't hold back. They're too honest.*

Simon: Everyone talks about the last throw of the final – 'God, that must have been difficult' – when in actual fact that was Steve's 'World Cup throw' – the best he had. The only rule when you throw more than fifteen metres is don't overthrow. Do that and you're in a world of difficulty because you've got a ball bouncing about in midfield. He didn't overthrow it, which allowed it to be caught. The view was the Australians wouldn't compete further than fifteen metres, so all he had to do was clear them beyond that distance.

Lewis: I knew where Steve was going to put that throw because by then I'd played with him for ages. There was no way the Aussie flanker George Smith was going to get it – he was too short – so it didn't really matter where it went so long as he got it to the back of the lineout.

Steve: *By that time, I definitely knew what I was doing in the lineout. However many balls Jonny Wilkinson kicked, I reckon I*

threw ten times more. You've heard of cauliflower ears? I've got
cauliflower elbows.

Robbo: Anything to seventeen metres he could hit really
well. Even so, for him to hit that last throw was truly
impressive. Also, nearly twenty years on, how often would a
hooker still be on the field to make that throw? Steve lasted
a hundred minutes no trouble at all.

Grays: Who plays a full game and extra time as a hooker?
Every second of it. Extraordinary!

Ben: He was so strong – he would go and go and go.

Clive: My starting position was that England would be the
fittest team in world rugby. I wanted them to be tough, but
more than anything they had to be aerobically fit. I had to
create what I called fifteen gold medal winners – one per
position. I would look at every team in the world and ask
if there was anybody who would get into my team, based
on the ability to run, really run, for eighty minutes. Some
of the fitness sessions were legendary, awesome, because the
competition for fitness was huge.

'If you can't play the whole game,' I said to them, 'you're
not in the team.' You can't bullshit players. They knew if
someone wasn't doing it, and if they weren't up to it, they
had to go.

Even now I'd say that team of 2003 was fitter than the

current one. Their levels were just fantastic, and Steve was as fit as they came. He was a great specimen in the gym, a monster. I was just glad he was on our team. If I'd seen him line up on the other side I'd have been thinking, *Oh no, we've got a bit of a beast here!* He just didn't slow down. He stayed fast and quick. I was never going to take Steve off a rugby pitch unless he was having a complete nightmare, which he never ever did.

Since then, the game has moved on. People are amazed now if a front rower stays on the whole game. If Steve was around today, he'd probably never play eighty minutes. He'd be subbed off with the rest of the front row, which I think is ridiculous, illogical. You go into rugby to play, not to sit on the bench. I can't think of anything worse than sitting on the bench. If I wasn't playing regularly, I'd just say, 'Forget it.'

Robbo: All the boys had worked really hard to get themselves so fit and into a position where they were playing in a World Cup final. At that point they had one opportunity. For the older players, great competitors like Neil Back, Jason Leonard and Martin Johnson, it was the last chance. They'd achieved with the Lions, with their clubs, but this was their last real chance to do it with England. Winning the final marked something special.

Clive: If we'd lost that World Cup final, I'd have never forgiven myself. We were the team to beat. I said to the players loads of times, 'Just look around this changing room. Is there any other room you'd rather be in? Would you rather be in the All Blacks' changing room? We're ahead of them in every way we're doing this.'

Someone would have had to play very well to beat us and, from a coaching point of view, that's a great position to be in. Sport is sport, and we could have lost that day, but we didn't, because we got so much right, especially selection.

Steve: *I saw Clive as the chief exec, making sure everything was absolutely bang on, overseeing every level of his plan being put into action.*

Clive: I'm not sure about 'chief exec'. I see myself more as conducting the orchestra! What's for sure is I wanted my time coaching England to be different from my time playing for England. I look back at my playing career and, while I'm obviously massively proud to have played twenty-one times for my country, if I'm honest it's also hugely disappointing, because we never really had an exciting team. We fundamentally played like everyone expected England to play. The ball came to the number 10 and he hoofed it up in the air. I spent half my playing career running along trying to catch the ball out of the sky. I'd been moaning about the way England played ever since I'd done it. I'd found watching England quite dull. I'd found playing for England quite dull. When I got the coaching job, it was a real moment for me to look in the mirror and say, 'Right, you've either got to put up or shut up.' I talked to the players so many times about having 80,000 people on their feet going nuts by the way we play. We weren't going to be doing that just by scrums and lineouts. We had to go to a whole new level.

'For this period in our lives,' I told the players, 'we're going to throw everything at this. We're going to play in a way that win, lose or draw we will walk off that pitch and go, "Wow! That was amazing!"' And that's what we achieved. I'm hugely proud that we won the World Cup, but even more so about the way we played. That starts with selection. You can have all these wonderful ways of doing things, but first of all you have to pick a team capable of carrying them out. The first rule is, don't look at the players you've got. Do that, and you'll end up playing like England normally play. I had an idea about every position. I was trying to do something totally different, and we achieved that.

Simon: When the final whistle went, Steve gave me the best compliment I've ever had. He came over to me, thanked me, and said he'd never have made it without me. When you think of everything that was going on at that point, all that excitement, emotion, players running around congratulating each other, for him to do that was exceptional.

Lewis: At the end, I specifically looked for Thommo. He was hugging Jason Leonard and I jumped on both of them.

By the time we'd left the stadium after doing all the press and TV stuff it was one in the morning. We'd arranged to meet at a bar at Sydney Harbour for a few drinks but it was so late that it ended up being a pretty quiet night compared to some I'd spend with Thommo. One in particular, after we played Ireland in Dublin in 2005, sticks in the memory. We were in the VIP room of a bar and next thing I knew a young Rory McIlroy had come over – he's a massive rugby fan. The next time I saw Rory, Thommo had him in a headlock. He was ruffling his hair like he was a little child. The VIP room was upstairs and I have a recollection of Steve dangling Rory over the balcony.

Steve: *I don't know about the balcony, but I did give Rory a big love bite, which prompted him to tweet to Matt Dawson – 'I hate Steve Thompson, that fat hooker of yours. He's given me a hickie! How do I explain that one when I get home!?'*

Robbo: Steve always enjoyed himself with the other players, but after that World Cup victory he never wanted the limelight that came some of the others' way. Rugby, and his success at it, enabled him to accept himself as a person. That's what I loved about him – he was who he was.

Steve: *I'm happy in the background. Despite the good looks, TV has never really been my thing.*

Grays: He never went after any attention. You make your own choices whether you like that kind of thing or not. He never traded on his name, he just enjoyed playing. He just quietly and unassumingly went about his business. It shouldn't be forgotten he was absolutely world class – for a period of time the best player in the world. He should be held up as one of the all-time greats.

Clive: Because we had such an exceptional pack of forwards, I don't think Steve got enough recognition. Not only did he become the best hooker in the world, he did so from a starting point of not really knowing how to throw at a lineout. He wasn't as high profile as Dallaglio or Johnson, but he was just as important – quite simply because if we lost him he was irreplaceable, whereas the other two weren't. This is why I love Steve Thompson – you can have all the ideas, but you need the players. One of my favourite sayings is: 'Great teams are made of great individuals.' While rugby is a fantastic team sport, fundamentally it's about every individual becoming the very, very best. It has to be because there are so many contrasting positions. The way Steve Thompson has to play compared to Matt Dawson or Jonny Wilkinson is very different. It's not like football where fundamentally everyone's the same size and plays in a similar way.

No two ways about it, Steve was absolutely fundamental to us winning the World Cup. He never let me down, ever. He was special, which is why I'm so sad at the situation he finds himself in now.

I hope he enjoyed being in the England team at that time, because of the way we played. I could think of nothing worse than Steve Thompson writing a book and saying he found it really boring playing under Clive Woodward!

Steve: *You're OK, Clive. By the sound of your words and everyone else's, the experience was epic from first to last. Winning the World Cup is meant to be an absolute highlight of any player's life, and it seems to have been exactly that.*

Thing is, knowing what I know now, I one hundred per cent wish it had never happened.

Chapter 4

THE LOST LION

L ife, as they say, is all about sliding doors. If I'd come along a few months later I wouldn't have been part of that World Cup squad, same as if I hadn't grown up in Northampton, I'd never have found rugby. Is that good luck? Or would the real luck have been if those doors had stayed shut? Had I continued along the line a couple more stops I would have had a totally different life. It wouldn't have contained the achievement, the glory. It could actually have been quite hard. But I might have been able to remember it.

It's the lack of any emotional bond that really upsets me. Not just England – I have an old shirt from the British & Irish Lions tour to New Zealand in 2005. Unfolding it recently gave me a jolt. I'd spent so much time trying to remember the World Cup that this was the first time I'd ever really considered whether I recalled my time with the Lions. But again, instead of fond memory there was a void. In 2005, I was, apparently, the best hooker across the four nations that make up that historic side. I say 'apparently' because I've no idea whether I was or not. I might as well have been looking at the shirt of a different player entirely.

I felt the same emptiness a few months later when Lewis, who was also on that trip, put an old squad photo on social media. I had no idea where it was taken, when it was taken. Lewis has spoken passionately of the camaraderie and brotherhood of the Lions, the uniqueness of players from rival nations putting past grievances aside to come together in a common cause. It should make the hairs on the back of my neck stand up. Instead I have complete disassociation. To all intents and purposes my time with the Lions never happened.

I do know I was vice-captain for a good part of that trip. I've read it – it's there in black and white – so it must have happened. Ireland skipper Brian O'Driscoll had originally led the tour but lasted just two minutes of the first Test before New Zealand captain Tana Umaga and hooker Keven Mealamu chose to lift him from the floor and pile-drive him into the ground. Brian could have suffered a horrific neck injury but managed to swivel just enough to take the impact through his shoulder. The subsequent dislocation ended his tour and so Alfie – Gareth Thomas – took the armband. Alfie was like a Messiah to the Welsh boys whereas we'd never actually met. As the new captain, he was entitled to choose his number two. According to Alfie, it was my reaction to defeat in that first Test that made him look in my direction. We were completely outplayed and afterwards Phil Larder was laying into us, criticising the forwards' reaction to New Zealand breaking through us. He felt we'd been too quick to rush back inside to help. At that point something just went inside me.

'That's bollocks,' I said. 'We reacted how anyone would react – we got back to look after our teammates. That's what you do. And I make no apologies for that.'

It was on the back of that little outburst that Alfie asked for me to be his vice-captain. It seemed that my values of looking after one another matched his own – an attitude forged in the changing rooms of amateur club rugby which we'd both so valued and enjoyed. I had no idea then how tortured inside Alfie was about his sexuality and the battles he was facing in his mind.

There's another incident from that tour that Lewis likes to remind me about. For no reason anyone could really understand, Tony Blair's former spin doctor Alastair Campbell was on the trip. Officially, he was 'head of communication', but this was rugby not Number 10. It wasn't Alastair's fault, but he was a fish out of water. Sadly, success on a Lions tour is not something that can be achieved through spin. On one occasion he was foolish enough to leave his BlackBerry unattended for a second. I took the chance to snaffle it. It was only a joke but Alastair was panic-stricken, desperately trying to get the device back off me. You can understand his anxiety – imagine the numbers of all those world leaders on there, all those private messages, emails, everything. I thought I'd make him sweat a little, but within minutes our head of security knocked on my hotel room door. Alastair had asked him to tell me that the UK secret services generally take a dim view of government phones being nicked and it might be a good idea to give it back. I didn't fancy a visit from the spooks in the middle of the night and so I duly handed it over.

◈

Sixteen years on, and at the start of the Lions tour to South Africa in 2021, I saw some coverage of the shirt presentations to the new members of the team. It occurred to me that the same thing must have happened to me and, as ever, I couldn't remember it. Some things just trigger my emotions, and this was one of them. I started crying, really upset. *I must have done that, must have had a shirt presentation. Someone special must have presented it to me. Everyone must have clapped. Why can't I remember any of it? Why can't I at least have that?* Like the World Cup, another huge moment gone.

It's at such times that, denied wallowing in nostalgia, I find myself drowning in anger. I try to remember what it was like, how it felt to pull on that jersey, to be part of something so iconic, and, aside from a few hazy images, flickering like an ancient cine-reel, realise I might as well not have been there. I start to hate the game. I don't want to turn into a hater. It's the worst thing I can do. Get into that frame of mind and I end up going down, down, down, into the depths.

Until that invasion of thoughts, I'd been looking forward to watching the first Lions Test. In the end I had a day out in Blackpool with the family. It was the best thing I could have done. We played on the beach, did the arcades, had fish and chips, and then drove down the prom with Seren hanging out the window gawping in disbelief at all the blokes dressed up as women for the never-ending parade of stag dos. Looking at her face in the rear-view mirror, I was reminded of how precious everything around me is. The past may be lost but the present most definitely isn't. And that, not rugby, is where I find my solace.

Chapter 5

BULIMIA

Talent and hard work got me into that Lions team and to the World Cup final. But I had another weapon in my armoury – bulimia.

I was sixteen when I first deliberately threw up my food. That was the age I became truly aware of my need for fitness, and that, for a person of my build, it was a battle that was never going to be easy to win. I've always loved my food and so to reduce my intake drastically enough to achieve peak performance weight was very hard. I don't remember the details of the very first time I made myself chuck up after a meal but I do know it soon became a matter of routine. I'd eat something I shouldn't, or what I considered too much, be overwhelmed by guilt, find the nearest toilet, and back it would all come. The smell of sick on my hands at training would disgust me.

I understand this sounds like absolute madness, not to mention totally foul, but when you're being pushed to be fitter and fitter, more and more physically able, then it's not hard to get into a mindset of *food's my problem, so get rid of it*. As an amateur, once I reached a decent level of fitness, I did actually stop the vomiting for a while, but when the sport went professional and the fitness staff were constantly on my back, especially with England, I soon slipped back into the old ways. For me, fat was always hanging around in the background. I've never been lucky enough to have natural fitness. I've always had to work at it. No matter how much training I did, I'd put weight on just like that. Even now, take my foot off the gas and the pounds soon start piling on. For a modern hooker that just doesn't work. Fitness is key for the team. You can't get away with just being big. If you can't get around the pitch, you're not being effective.

To address my attractiveness to the forces of blubber, I did extra training in secret. Away from prying eyes, I'd put myself through the mill doing endless fat-burning routines at the gym. If I then went out and had a curry with friends, I knew it would undo all the good work and so when I got home, I'd just heave it all out again. I never thought there was anything wrong with doing that. It was simply a practical way of dealing with it; a way of having the best of all worlds, enjoying food, enjoying friendships, and not wrecking all the fitness work. I know it's not normal, but in some ways it's like the dementia – when you're living it, you're not actually aware of what normality is, or the fact you've slipped so far outside of it.

My obsession with weight was instilled in me by both club and country. Every second I was on the pitch, Saints wanted premium me. To achieve that, I ended up in a one-man 'fat club', undergoing a totally different fitness regime to other players. In the run-up to the World Cup, England, meanwhile, would weigh my food, literally everything that went in my mouth, even salad. I did have the odd trick up my sleeve. At breakfast, for instance, at a training camp or in a hotel, after I'd had my oats and milk, I'd occasionally take a little trip round the buffet. I'd eat a few sausages, the odd slice of bacon, a bit of scrambled egg cooked in cream. I convinced myself that if it wasn't on my plate then calories didn't count. I know – I was only playing games with myself. On top of that I'd be forever trying different diets, thinking they were the next great thing, only to be bored senseless with them in a few days.

In the end, despite being in environments where food was readily available and plentiful, I came to see I didn't need that much. While I'd watch other players enjoying a big sit-down lunch and then later, at the end of training, huge plates of proper nice sandwiches, all washed down with sugar-drenched energy drinks, I found I could live on virtually nothing. I hardly touched the food and just drank water. Occasionally, though, I'd binge eat. I'd be strict with my intake but then, if there was something in front of me I really liked, I'd go for it. Feeling overfull, or a bit guilty, I'd then head to the toilet and stick my fingers down my throat. My fat percentages were always at the back of my mind, and so it was only natural for me to think, *Right, that's got to come back out.* Sometimes I wouldn't eat all day. I'd train morning and afternoon, have a massive dinner, and then make myself sick. The Steve Thompson weight-loss plan, available in all bad bookshops.

I've seen ex-England cricketer Andrew Flintoff talk about his experience of bulimia, but while he went out of his way to keep his condition secret, I was actually known for it. If the lads were going out for some nice food, I wouldn't want to miss out. Afterwards, I'd openly say to them, 'Right, better get that lot out again.' They'd be laughing. They thought it was something I was doing every now and again, not as a matter of routine. I'd laugh, too. I knew what I was doing qualified as bulimia, that it wasn't right, but much more important to me was that I needed to be the right weight. Having a laugh about it somehow made it acceptable to all concerned.

There was another reason I couldn't keep it secret – I sound like a walrus when I'm throwing up. Honestly, you could stick me on the top of a cliff, make me eat a cream cake and use me as a foghorn.

Mental confusion for sportspeople over food and its value is understandable. When I started out, it was all carbs, carbs, carbs. At Northampton, we were piling through three massive bowls of pasta a day, which was a recipe for weight gain if ever there was one. Then, towards the end of my career, it was all change. Suddenly, aside from loading in the run-up to a game, carbs were off the menu. It was all fresh produce, fish, salad, that kind of thing. The result was a massive seesawing of weight. I would stand on the scales every single day. At the weekend I'd be 122 kilos. Then, immediately after the game, I'd have to get back down. If not, the weight would stay on and I'd just get bigger and bigger. By Tuesday I'd be around 116 kilos. I was in an impossible situation of trying to keep the weight on and trying to keep it off as well. It was one gigantic endless battle. I used throwing up as an effective weight-loss tool from the start to the finish of my career.

A nutritionist once told me my body type was that of a Samoan – I was naturally massive and there was only so much I could do about it. I knew what they meant. Northampton would put me on really strict diets, cut right back on my carbs, and still the weight would go on. If I did gym work and weights, I'd just get bigger. There were times I felt like a freak. Occasionally, we'd have a dose of sickness and diarrhoea shoot through the club. For someone like Matt Dawson, who'd battle for weeks to put weight on – muscle, not fat – it was a nightmare, because within forty-eight hours all that hard work had been undone. I, on the other hand, would be firing at both ends but also get the munchies. The other lads couldn't believe it – 'Steve, you're the only person who could get sickness and diarrhoea and put weight on!'

◈

I was never averse to extreme measures to address issues with my body. By the summer of 2006 I felt I was falling apart after playing relentlessly for years. While England travelled to Australia, I decided instead to head to Thailand to spend several days with a tube stuck up my backside. Colonic irrigation was being flagged up more and more as a way of flushing out and recharging the system, and by the time I checked out after this rather unusual break, having not consumed anything other than fruit smoothies for ten days, I'd lost seven kilos. However, it's a cruel trick that when you're a naturally big person, you often don't notice any physical difference.

It was Saints' Kiwi scrum half Mark Robinson who put me on to the retreat, and it sounded exactly what I needed, a complete physical and mental overhaul – basically a pre-preseason. I'd had so many injuries that if I was going to survive in the sport I needed a restart. I felt like a car driving on fumes. My psoriasis had got really bad, a major trigger for which is tiredness and stress, to the extent that my fellow pros had started calling me the 'red leopard'. I was flaking so much I carried a little handheld vacuum round with me. It wasn't enough for some of my teammates – 'Fuck off! You're not coming in my house!'

Coaches were forever saying, 'Make sure you leave everything out on the pitch.'

'Not a problem,' I'd say. 'I leave myself everywhere.'

A trip to Thailand to shove a tube up your arse would generally be a big-time source of piss-taking in rugby circles.

With most of the lads away over the summer, I was spared the worst and, in all honesty, it wouldn't have bothered me one bit anyway. It was what I wanted to do and that was all that mattered. It says everything for how much good those ten days did me that I can remember a fair bit of it, possibly because my brain was getting a recharge rather than a battering. With those rare points in my career where I did get a rest, it does seem a little easier to find tiny bits of memory.

Thing is, when I tell them about it most people really do wish this was one thing I really had forgotten.

For the colonic irrigation, I had to go up to a hut three times a day. In there was a bucket with coffee in the bottom, definitely not for drinking. I'd add hot water, hang the bucket up, lie on my back, legs akimbo, and feed a tube from the bucket up my back passage. Gravity would bring the liquid rushing down to its destination, at which point I'd rub my stomach and out it would all come again. Fortunately, it was before the fad for taking selfies.

At the start, the people who ran the retreat gave me a card which told me exactly what I could expect to come out of my backside on any given day. I didn't think much of it at the time but by day five, when I was looking at what appeared to be seaweed, I was grateful for the reassurance, as I was for the company of Michael Choi, a bass player and producer who'd worked with some big artists such as MIKA, Annie Lennox and Beth Ditto, who really helped me get through it. We had a daily routine – together we'd go to restaurants and watch people eat.

With the hunger element in mind, I could have chosen a better box set to take with me. Littered with the most amazing food, vast Italian family feasts, from start to finish, I very quickly started to wish I'd not packed *The Sopranos*.

The care I take over my weight and food now comes from a motivation very different from being effective at sport. In the morning, I'll have two bits of sourdough toast topped with almonds, then for lunch perhaps tuna and sweetcorn, and in the evening we'll cook a four-person meal for the six of us, which works because I won't have any of the carbs, replacing them with something simple like grated carrot. Typically, on this fairly meagre diet I still struggle to keep the weight off, even when combined with an exercise regime, but it's something I'll stick at because I know the importance of diet when fighting dementia. Leafy vegetables make a regular appearance on my plate as do berries, nuts, and fish high in omega-3 fatty acids, all said to help the brain stay healthy. I leave out cauliflower as it's like eating my ears.

Even now, though, I still occasionally make myself sick. There are certain foods, ribs and wings especially, I find very hard to resist. I'll overdo it, feel too full, a bit uncomfortable and go off to the toilet. But overall I have a much better relationship with food than in my playing days, eating sensibly at set times. Similarly, while I still work out, I'm not doing so as someone whose body is constantly being damaged, who needs to repair and build himself up. So much of my problem, mentally and physically, was that rugby in my era was all about size and strength. They made me so big when actually a player's effectiveness comes from power rather than size. As a player I was always treading a knife-edge between strength and agility and sometimes felt drastic measures were the only way I could possibly achieve the pay-off.

Equally, it could be argued that I've always had a dysfunctional relationship with food, that was just exaggerated by the extreme sporting world which I then entered. As a kid I ate as and when food was around, be it at home, school or friends' houses. As you'll see in the next chapter, I very definitely wasn't from a home where there was a good square meal on the table at a set time; where the family sat down at breakfast and politely enquired what the day might bring for each other. I grew up learning that food was functional. You filled up when you could on what you could and got on with life in between.

Yes, it wasn't great that I ended up being bulimic, but you have to remember that I never for one minute thought of it as a mental illness. If anything, I was happy to have found a solution that worked for me. It wasn't hurting anyone, including, I thought, myself. Of course, that's not true. Bulimia is not called an 'eating disorder' for nothing. Your stomach doesn't exist in isolation from your brain. But when you've grown up so independently you find your own way to make the world work.

Because of that, bulimia was – and still is a little bit – mine.

Chapter 6

EARLY DAYS

I never wanted to be a rugby player – winning the World Cup with England never featured in my dreams. I always fancied being a policeman. Surprising really, considering my early years weren't exactly spent on the straight and narrow. I very nearly got caught shoplifting at six years old. Me and my mate Richard would pinch marbles from the corner shop and flog them in the playground. Decent little earner that was, until the shopkeeper spotted us in the act. While Richard was collared, I showed a flash of early rugby promise by pushing past the bloke and running away. Gallantly, I let Richard take the flak – I don't think his mum ever forgave me. I'd like to say that brush with authority put an end to my pilfering ways, but I was a big lad with a sweet tooth. I switched from marbles to confectionery – 'pick 'n' nick', surely you've heard of it?

As a kid, it was just the usual stuff – ringing people's doorbells, waiting behind a hedge, and then egging them when they answered the door; getting a job delivering free newspapers and saving a bit of shoe leather by setting the lot on fire. I think it's fair to say I led Richard astray. But given my size – I'd hit five feet by the age of eight – I was probably a pretty decent person to hang around with. Richard, who lived a few doors down, was half my height. From his point of view, he had ready-made protection wherever he went.

I'd arrived in Richard's and a few other mates' lives by a rather circuitous route, parts of which even now remain a bit of a mystery. I was born in Hemel Hempstead but came to Northampton almost straight away. My mum and real dad split up when I was barely out of nappies and for some reason I went to live with my grandparents on my dad's side, near Cromer, which explains why I'm a Norwich City fan. My memory, dementia or no dementia, of those East Anglian days is hazy, but I have an underlying feeling it was a good point in my life, probably the most stable of my childhood. Then, just as I started school, I came back to Northampton to live with my mum. I would still see Dad, a policeman, occasionally, but he lived fifty miles away in Welwyn Garden City and over the next few years we lost touch until by the time I was ten he'd gone from my life. I would be twenty-two by the time I next met him, at which point the emotional and physical bond had been well and truly broken. When your dad comes back into your life after that long, it's never going to be like him being a dad as most people might think it. Instead, I just saw this huge bloke. As soon as I clapped eyes on him, I understood why, despite my love of the game, I was never destined to be a footballer.

As my dad slipped out of the picture, my mum got together with another bloke who adopted me, at which point I went from Steve Thompson to Steve Walter. I never liked my stepdad. We never got on and, despite the adoption, I never felt he wanted me around. Early in my rugby career, I changed my name back to Thompson. I didn't want to be associated with him in any way, shape or form.

We were living on the Blackthorn Estate in Northampton's Eastern District, one of the roughest areas of the town. Tough it might have been, but Blackthorn became my playground. Home, with its endless arguments and fraught atmosphere, was somewhere I never wanted to be, and so I spent every minute I could out of the house, messing about in the woods or playing any sport me and my mates could think of. If Wimbledon was on it would be tennis in the road. Other times I'd be kicking a football against the wall of an end house – Boom! Boom! Boom! Eventually the poor sods who lived there could take no more and would come out and go absolutely spare.

Most days I'd go out at seven in the morning and not come back until eleven at night, sometimes escaping the neighbourhood entirely to ride out to visit mates in surrounding villages on a BMX with no gears – I also had no helmet and no lights. It's funny seeing my own children now and thinking back to when I was a kid. I was walking to school on my own when I was five, out on my bike half the night when I was eight. No one had a clue where I was. No way would I let one of my kids out on their own at that age. Sometimes other kids would look at me – out at all hours, no discipline – and say to me, 'I wish I had a mum like yours because then I could do anything.' When they grew up a bit, they changed their tune: 'Thank God I had the mum and dad I did.'

Flitting from place to place, popping up unexpectedly here, there and everywhere, I was a ghost child. And like any ghost, there's practically zero evidence of me ever existing. I've been asked a few times for pictures of myself from when I was a small kid or a teenager, and there aren't any. It just never happened. Whether my mum had a camera back then I couldn't say, but even had I positioned myself in front of the lens I'm pretty sure she'd have pointed it away. My mate Hephs – Simon Hepher, who also made it as a pro rugby player, and a bloke who to this day I consider a brother – mentions a time when she deliberately locked me out of the house late at night. She was in there but just wouldn't let me in. I rang Hephs and he came over and found me sitting against a wall at the side of the road.

I know that's a pretty miserable image but before you start reaching for the Kleenex, I'll tell you this – I never thought about it like that at the time. That kind of thing was my normal. And anyway, I always had my guard up. As a kid I wouldn't show emotion – ever. Around Blackthorn you soon learned not to show any weakness. Compare that to now. These days I cry over anything. Me and Steph will be watching *Britain's Got Talent* and I'll be filling up, hand over my face trying not to let her see. Things get to me in a way they never used to. I know having a young family can often make people more emotional, but I do feel like my character is softening. I went to a friend's wedding recently. He was marrying a Polish girl and her dad didn't speak a word of English, and yet he'd gone to the effort of writing out this incredibly moving speech in a language he didn't know. Add that to the sight of him getting up in front of a load of strangers to deliver those incredibly heartfelt words and I was totally welling up. But as a kid? Forget it. Crying was a complete no-no.

I knew I was seen as a bit of a rough kid, but I wasn't alone in coming from a less than ideal background and I was luckier than some in that other kids' parents used to look out for me. They'd have me round for Sunday lunch and were so kind and considerate that often it felt like I was part of their families. I loved that at the time, and always tried to be well-mannered, but there's part of me now that worries about whether I was taking the piss by hanging around. I hope not, because I really did appreciate their generosity, their attempts to make up for the lack of stability I was experiencing at home. Blood's thicker than water? Not for me it isn't. Water, not blood, was what kept me going. I look back at Hephs' parents and those of other kids and use them as role models – that's how I want to be with my own children now.

◈

Sport, proper organised sport, began to offer a welcome distraction. Bizarrely, it was roller skating that first got me noticed. It's not 1 April as I write this, so please believe me when I tell you that the big lummox you saw on the rugby field was actually British roller speed-skating champion when he was ten, finishing sixth in the European Championships in Germany. A friend loved the sport and dragged me down to practice to have a go. I'd never been on skates but I was winning right from the start and within eight months was national champion, performing at outdoor velodromes across the country and skating between fifteen and twenty miles a night, four nights a week around the park in Northampton. There was even talk of converting me to ice and fast-tracking me into the Olympic team. But, while seeing myself in a write-up in the local paper was nice, I was far more interested in football and after a year or so hung up my wheels. I was equally glad to hang up, or possibly incinerate, my Lycra bodysuit, something I was never likely to look good in, even then.

I was fortunate that the school I attended, Blackthorn Middle, fed into Northampton School for Boys, known for its great record academically and renowned for being equally excellent for sport. While I had no interest in the first, I definitely did in the second, and from the minute I set foot in the school loved the sheer amount and variety of sport on offer. Basketball became my first love and I was selected to play for the Midlands. I was never the most talented player on court but my height and speed made me a threat, as did my desire. I wanted the ball more than anybody. I fought and fought, kept on going. That determination was why I kept getting picked, although the coach did once bawl me out for being what he considered overly physical.

'You're more like a rugby player than someone who plays basketball,' he bellowed. He might have had a point there.

As a footballer, I played centre back in the county side a few times. To be a pro was my absolute dream. Of course, that never happened, but I did actually make one televised appearance, in the Alan Ball Memorial Cup, an England versus The World celebrity and legends tribute match to the World Cup winner after he died in 2007. The commentators said I was the best non-footballer on the field, although since Vernon Kay was also appearing maybe that wasn't saying a great deal.

However, as I got older and filled out, the PE department decided my size and pace was definitely made for the oval ball. This was news to me. While Northampton was very much a rugby town, I had never followed its professional club, the Saints, always being more interested in football and basketball. When I had been dragged down to Franklin's Gardens by a mate, my first impression of rugby was that, while I was big and fast and so ideally suited to it, it was a game you'd have to be mad to play. It just seemed so full-on, hard and complicated. And that was before I found out they all showered together.

I was fifteen by the time I actually started playing and I'm sure even then I'd have never seriously pursued it were it not for my first coach at school, Mark Lee. Mark and his PE colleague Pete 'Snapper' Dewsnap spotted the ingredients – size, speed, handling skills, never-say-die attitude – that together made a recipe for success. Right from the start Mark encouraged me, instilling in me that if I worked hard and listened I could achieve something special. He could also see that a background in basketball wasn't a bad thing – ball handling skills and hand-to-eye coordination were transferable.

Together, Mark and Pete were phenomenal. 'Snapper', in particular, wasn't to be messed with – one of those teachers who could silence a roomful of noisy kids merely with his presence. But while others cowered in his wake, I loved him – I didn't just need that discipline, I was crying out for it. Mark, meanwhile, displayed methods of coaching that were nothing if not original. Refereeing one game, and wanting me to carry the ball forward, he gave a penalty against me for running sideways with it tucked under one arm. Strangely, I still recall his exact words: 'Walter! It's not an underarm deodorant you know.' To the bemusement of the other side, he'd do the same if he felt I'd travelled too far without making a pass. Eventually, Mark would lay off the whistle and give me free rein to run with the ball. Let off the leash I'd grab the chance to score a few tries.

Mark might have felt the need to teach me a few lessons, but one thing he never interfered with was what would become one of my trademarks, what he calls my 'dog work ethic', my willingness to scramble on the ground, to be down in the mud doing the unseen stuff. I'd never been given something for nothing, had scrapped for everything, and didn't see sport as being any different. No matter how tough the situation I was never going to give in. If my childhood had taught me anything it was to keep going and going until eventually, from somewhere, anywhere, you get a break. I'm not saying a tough background is the only source of competitiveness. After all, one of my best mates is Lewis Moody, who had pretty much everything on a plate as a kid, and he's one of the most competitive people I know. The difference with Lewis, though, is he's daft. Therefore, he'd do anything, just keep going and going – even when he didn't have to. The only question was if he'd notice the referee had blown the final whistle and everyone had gone home. In my case, though, I'm sure my edge, my desire, that chip on the shoulder about what I saw as my competitors' easy path through life, made me want to prove myself. I wanted to stick two fingers up at those who doubted someone like me could succeed, and that's what drove me to invest a hundred per cent in everything I did as a rugby player. So Mark was right. I was never going to be one of those glory-seekers sliding across the grass trying to look good for the cameras. I was going to be a battler. I was going to do anything to come out on top.

I took notice of Mark because I believed in him as a person as well as someone who knew rugby inside out. I also took notice because he gave me no choice. 'You'd better listen to me, Steve Walter,' he'd say, 'because I'm the best coach you're ever going to have.' When I look back on the coaches

I've played under, legends such as Wayne 'the Professor' Smith and Ian McGeechan, I always tell people Mark Lee was the best – because he told me he was.

The fact I placed so much weight on Mark's words made his statement after one game – 'You'll play for England' – quite incredible. Mark wasn't one to throw around praise willy-nilly. He says he's only ever said that about three players in his life. What he saw in me was physicality, work ethic, good hands and athletic ability. Even so, I still wasn't wholly convinced that rugby was the sport in which I wanted to invest everything. At one point I actually knocked on Mark's office door and told him I wanted to give it up. Basketball, I insisted, was the game for me. We managed to find a compromise. For a year I'd play both and then make a decision. In no time I was training twice a week with the rugby team, while still playing basketball. I also joined Northampton Old Scouts, a fantastic rugby club whose pitches were next to the school playing fields, and where I first encountered a gangly youth called Ben Cohen, little knowing the journey we were about to embark on together would take in a certain night in Sydney a decade or so later.

Bit by bit, basketball inched its way on to the backburner and rugby became the absolute dominant presence in my life. I played Saturdays and Sundays and, with zero help from my mum and stepdad getting to and from games, I organised myself. I'd ride my bike, get the bus or hope other parents would help. A lot of them did just that. Taking pity on me because of my shambolic home life, knowing I'd had a bit of a rough time, they could see I was good at rugby and wanted to encourage it. As well as lifts to games they'd pick me up after training so I could hang out round theirs for a bit.

By now I was mixing in a few different circles – school friends, pals round where I lived, rugby mates, and then what you might call 'bad influences', by which I mean people older than me who went out nicking and generally getting up to no good. Weirdly, considering my own upbringing, I always knew right from wrong and so never went the same way. It helped that I was never particularly anti-authority. While I wasn't averse to blowing up the odd dog-shit bin with the help of a packet of matches and an aerosol, I had no interest in going down a more hardcore criminal route, stealing cars, robbing houses, dealing drugs. I'd watch people take or smoke something and then just sit there zombified, staring at the stereo. I could never see the appeal and no more wanted a slice of that than I did to break into someone's house, something which sickened me because I could well imagine the hurt it would cause.

There was part of me that always turned away from the wrong path. Occasionally, I'd be faced with some lad or other intent on proving themselves the hardest on the estate, turning their sights on me because of my size. In their heads there was no better way of showing their strength than by taking on the big lad who looked five years older than anyone else, but I thought they were idiots. I never wanted anything to do with that kind of nonsense. It was plain stupid and didn't interest me in the least. On one occasion, me and Richard walked into the shopping centre and a group of lads started having a go. Richard, half my size, certainly wasn't interested in a fight. We both ran off and spent a very uncomfortable half hour lying flat on top of a garage in hiding.

That's not to say I was the most angelic student ever to walk through the doors of Northampton School for Boys – in fact, I'm sure I was quite difficult – but I enjoyed it, found drive and focus and did my best to learn. With my home life a disaster, school was a welcome refuge. I never wanted to play truant. I couldn't understand that attitude – why would you want to wag off when you could be at school with your mates? In the end, however, I was perhaps a little too – shall we say, 'energetic'? – and got kicked out for scrapping. Later, when I went on to play for England, it made me laugh that the school couldn't get me back quickly enough to do a talk.

'The difference now,' I told the pupils, 'is that this school offers something for everybody. Whatever their strength. Not just sport but music, art, drama and 101 other things as well – it gives that person an avenue to go down and back it up.' The proof is in the pudding – Matt Smith, the former Doctor Who, went to Northampton School for Boys.

While school might have disappeared, rugby remained. I've heard it said that some people enjoy contact sports because it's a great way of them diverting the anger they felt as a child. Let's face it, there's not many middle-class boxers, are there? I never felt like that. For me, I excelled at a contact sport because I just happened to be good at it and had natural athleticism on my side. OK, you need drive to reach the top in sport, but for me rugby was the easy thing to do, a lot easier, I'm sure, than a lot of other jobs out there, working in hospitals, emptying bins, being out on the streets dealing with criminals – the everyday jobs that so few people appreciate or even see. You could say I was lazy choosing rugby. Certainly, I never loved the game like I did football and basketball. If I did have a subconscious attachment to the sport, it was because it was providing me with something I'd never had – a family. I had the tools to play the game, and in return it gave me friendship, togetherness, protection and loyalty.

I know for sure that rugby saved me at a time when what might laughably be termed 'family life' finally came to an end. When I was seventeen, out of the blue, my mum and stepdad kicked me out. There'd been no big run-ins or anything like that, but one teatime they turned to me and told me, 'We want you gone.' I shouldn't have been surprised. They'd done the same to my older half-sister a few years earlier. I didn't argue. They weren't worth it, and it wasn't like I hadn't been looking out for myself for years anyway. I just got a few things together, chucked them in the back of an old Vauxhall Nova I'd bought, and went. I've never spoken to either of them since.

◈

Getting away from 'home' was one of the best things I ever did. By the time I left, there were a few houses in the immediate neighbourhood where people would hide out from the police. Just as me and a mate were getting in the Nova one day, this Scottish bloke appeared. He was drunk, aggressive and put a gun to our heads. Because of my background, it didn't seem that odd to me. It was just the kind of stupid stuff that happened round there. In fact, I was laughing as he did it. But for my mate, who wasn't from the area, it was a massive shock. The whole thing, as I could have told him, came to nothing and was over as quickly as it had started. But who knows how remaining in that environment would have affected me without the discipline and security of rugby? Maybe one day I'd have been the one hiding from the police.

I'd started college after school, with thoughts of training to be a chippy, but leaving home put me in a spot financially and so I started earning a few quid doing odd jobs here and there, including my burgeoning career as a doorman. I'd begun working the pubs and clubs of Northampton from the age of sixteen – my size made me look older than most of the people trying to get in. Mention the word 'doorman' and people immediately think of punch-ups and brawls, but in those days there was never actually that much trouble. Northampton is like a village in that if you're out and about you get to know everyone pretty quickly. If anyone did get in your face, you'd just grab them and chuck them out. It also counted that I was from the Eastern District – that alone would put most people off from having a go.

More than anything it was drugs we were looking out for. One time I was working the door of an event at Northampton

Guildhall. This lad was queuing and I could tell straight away he was hiding something. He was nervous, shifty. I had a look in his fag packet and it turned out he'd taken all the tobacco out of his cigarettes, filled the gaps with Ecstasy tablets, and then stuffed the tobacco back in to hide them. When he saw I'd rumbled him he was absolutely devastated. That was his way of earning a few quid and I'd taken it off him. I called the police over, they bagged up his stash and off he went.

Most people, though, were just out on the booze. It would make me laugh to see how their characters would change over the course of an evening. In Northampton, there's the Wellingborough Road, or 'the Welly' as it's known locally. At one point there were eighteen pubs down there, perfect for a game of 'pub golf', a different drink in each one, before ending up in the town centre. Alternatively, you could do it the other way round, which meant starting at The Wedgwood, where I worked on the door. At this stage, the blokes I'd meet would be the nicest you could imagine. Several hours later, however, when I encountered them again, this time working on the door at Stirling's nightclub, named after the RAF bomber that crashed on the town in 1941, they'd have turned into slobbering, incomprehensible madmen. A week later they'd see me back at The Wedgwood – 'Sorry about last week, mate' – before starting the whole horrendous ritual all over again. Some people thought I was missing out on my own social life by working the doors. I never saw it like that. At Christmas and New Year, for example, because there was always a lot of rugby fixtures, I didn't want to drink anyway.

All the lads were going out getting drunk while I was earning rather than spending and still having a laugh with my mates on the doors.

The other security guys tended to be older than me, colourful characters – one of them broke into the cash boxes of rural telephone kiosks with a diamond-tipped drill. That, and the door money, was how he made his living. At times it felt like being in an East Midlands mafia, a little bit gangland, with rival firms chasing the same business. At one point I was headhunted by another outfit. The gear alone was worth the switch – blue dicky-bow and a long black gangster coat. I loved it – in Northampton there weren't many opportunities to dress up like you were on a film set. The switch, however, didn't go down well with the head of the crew I had previously been working for. My old boss saw me in town and beckoned for me to follow him round a corner. Out of sight he punched me hard in the stomach. I just stood there and took it. He had a couple of other boys with him and it wasn't worth the hassle. A few years later, after I'd played for England, I bumped into him and we had a good laugh about it.

'Why did you do it?' I asked him.

'Reputation,' he replied. 'I couldn't be seen just to have people leaving me.' I could have pointed out it was Northampton not New York but decided to let it lie.

Working for the new firm meant secret Sunday meetings in an old nightclub above a bowling alley. The doormen would gather before the boss turned up. On arrival, he'd walk round and press cash into our palms as he shook our hands. It was all very Al Capone, which a lot of the blokes liked – there were some naughty boys down there.

Ben Cohen's dad, Peter, was a big part of me turning my back on that slightly shady world. He would do anything to help out at the Old Scouts, be it giving lifts to games, sorting refreshments or just being there to give us support. Peter had worked in the nightclub business and told me I should stop working the doors. He didn't think it was good for me in the long run to be in that environment, words which would come flooding back to me a few years later when, awfully, he died after a violent attack in a nightclub in the town.

I looked up to Peter – he was a friend as well as a mate's dad – and saw straight away that he was right. My fellow doormen, and the worlds they inhabited, were the complete opposite to the coaches who were transforming my life. I encountered Kiwi Matt Bridge at school and then again as I started to fly within the radar of Saints, where as a youth coach he helped a lot of youngsters find a foothold in the professional game. At that stage, while I had potential, I was lacking some personal discipline on the fitness front. I ate too much and had found a liking for beer. Matt could see how slipping down that route could put a full stop to my progress and came hard at me in an attempt to make me see sense. He would make me do endless runs. I found them incredibly hard and would sometimes collapse to the floor or even be sick. If I did get to play, he would only give me ten minutes at the end. I confronted him about it.

'How come I'm only getting ten minutes?'

'Because ten minutes is all you can give me,' he replied. 'Give me more and you'll get more.' Tough love I think you'd call it. But Matt was also keenly aware of my psychology. He'd laid down a challenge and knew I was someone who would always battle to the end to prove a detractor wrong.

I put in the hard yards and it paid off as I began getting regular starts. Matt, and Keith Picton, the team manager, really began to mould me into the player I would become. Matt saw me as a close-quarter combat fighter and began to play me as a prop, while Keith, as well as being a fantastic coach, became like a dad to me. From the moment I got down to Saints he was constantly looking after me. Early on we went over to play Gloucester at their Kingsholm ground. We played out of our skins and scored a last-minute try to win. A great achievement and an incredible feeling with a fantastic bunch of lads. Keith had a little joke he'd play, where on the way back from a game he'd stop the minibus at a chip shop and make us each eat a pickled egg. Thankfully, we would also have fish and chips to take the taste away. We called in at a chippy in Gloucester before we hit the road proper. The boys all got off the bus – except me.

'Go on, Wally,' Keith said to me. 'Go and get your food.'

'It's OK. I'm good.'

'Don't be daft.'

'Seriously, I'm all right.'

'You haven't got any money, have you?'

I was embarrassed, head down. Keith always had a little float. He gave me a fiver. 'Go and join your mates.' To anyone else that might just seem like a bloke handing out a fiver. To me, it was massive.

Keith would take this a step further when Saints announced a development tour for young and upcoming players to America. No way could I afford to go, and so he went straight out and got me sponsored.

But Keith, who played a massive part in the development of many Saints players, such as Matt Dawson, was no soft touch. The lads would all have a drink on the way back from an away game, and, with no toilet on board, would use the empties to piss in. Inevitably, there were spillages and if Keith thought I needed a bit of a kick up the arse, which wasn't unusual, he'd make me stay behind to clean it up. His message was always clear – yes, I had talent, yes, I could get somewhere in the game, but it was never going to come off if I didn't take it seriously and give my everything in trying to make it happen. He looked out for me when I was a proper rough diamond and made me believe that if I didn't give it my best shot I'd be missing out on an incredible future. Even when I made it into the England ranks, he kept pushing, refusing to come to my early games. 'You're that good, you'll play fifty games for England,' he told me. 'So when you play your fiftieth, I'll come to that.'

More than anything, Keith, and Matt, gave me boundaries. The message was simple – 'Do whatever you want within those boundaries, but if you stray outside it's all over.' I thrived on that. For the first time in my life I had something like a solid framework to support me. Those parameters were effectively my parents. By no means is it stretching it to say I looked at Keith as a father figure.

I also knew I was very good at rugby and that maintaining this new feeling of solidity depended on me building on that. I had no intention of being one of those people who looked back at a missed opportunity. I wanted to fulfil my potential. That's not to say I turned into a choirboy. Far from it. I still had a lot of energy and was still very strong-willed. Sometimes to drill the message home, people had to be blunt with me. At that stage, had a coach put an arm round my shoulders and been all sweetness and light, I'd have just taken the piss, whereas if someone was harder with me, and there was two-way respect, I'd give them everything.

When I started playing for East Midlands Under-19s with Saints coach Alan Hughes, he definitely understood that about me. Early on in our relationship, I pulled my hamstring but travelled on the team bus to an away game anyway. I was messing around at the back, which culminated in me jumping out the fire door when we arrived. Alan went absolutely mad, telling me how I was letting everyone down, myself included. I completely focused from that point on. We soon developed a great understanding and he came to realise that just because I might occasionally greet him by sticking my tongue in his ear it didn't mean I had anything other than one hundred per cent respect for him and his methods. Similarly, I knew that if he was driving me particularly hard in training he was only doing so because he wanted me to make the absolute best of myself.

Alan also recognised I had an edge about me and reiterated that, without discipline, aggression means nothing. But, while it might not have always seemed that way, I knew that already. While I had a short fuse at times and wouldn't take any shit from anybody, I was always in control. Like any good player, I didn't want people to get the better of me, which meant that throughout my career, whenever I trained, it didn't matter who I was up against – best mate or anything – I'd have taken their head off if it meant delivering a true representation of what I and they would face on the pitch. That fighting spirit led some people to say I was a nutter. The truth was I was actually honing my desire to win to the ultimate degree, always investing in what I could deliver. I only got sent off once in my entire rugby-playing life, and that was a school match, class versus class. The opponent who caused me to boil over was my best mate. He knee-dropped me (which he still denies), so I got up and levelled him. He ran off with me in pursuit – I'd have killed him if I'd got hold of him – and we were both dismissed. From that point on, I played with self-discipline. Once I realised how big a part respect and manners play in rugby, controlling yourself on and off the pitch, it was something I totally bought into. Weird really – manners and respect were never instilled in me by my parents, but people have always complimented me on them. 'We always knew if you were out with our son, you'd look after him,' they tell me, looking back to those early days. 'You were always very polite even though we knew you were a wrong'un.'

With that East Midlands team, a group of players and coaches I really loved, I properly started going places. Two years running we reached the Under-19s County Championship final, held on the biggest stage of all, Twickenham, and won both times. Alan used me as a back- row forward in the first final, before graduating to loosehead prop for the second.

Actually, the East Midlands glory years could have ended before they'd barely begun. Two weeks before our first final I fell out the back of a mate's van at twenty miles an hour. I expect the road came off worst. Even so, I badly bruised an elbow and knee. Fair to say, Alan wasn't best pleased, although not in the least surprised. By then he'd got used to the fact that Steve Walter and the odd scrape went hand in hand. He saw me as rugby's Artful Dodger, as full-on and in-your-face as I was vulnerable; perhaps not quite as confident as I liked to make out. Like those other coaches before him, he understood full well that rugby had filled a void in my life. He knew that the hard and unyielding Steve was actually a bit of a façade. He also treated me as being old enough to make my own mistakes, never talking down to me, and seeing the entire squad as young adults, which we were. We would have a beer after a match, and the coaches would come with us. They enjoyed our company as much as we enjoyed theirs. Never did any of those coaches who worked with me in my youth judge me. In rugby, it wasn't uncommon to encounter the odd snob in a blazer, people who seemed to feel you weren't worthy unless you came from a certain school, a certain background. I was fortunate enough always to be around people who not only took me as I came but embraced me for it.

For all the success I would go on to have, World Cup winner included, playing for East Midlands is the most treasured part of my career. Nothing else compares. I don't have to reach deep into my mind for the happiest I ever felt in a rugby shirt, because I know that first Under-19s final against Hertfordshire was never bettered. At that point everything came together – Twickenham, underdogs, an amazing bunch of mates playing for each other. What we achieved as a group, a bunch of amateurs, was incredible. As a professional, I was a hired gun, a paid assassin. For that reason, any achievement can never have the same meaning, the same emotion, as succeeding with a bunch of players who turn up because they love the game, the team and the craic.

Where the amateur and the professional are linked is that, having smelled a little bit of success, I was driven to take my career forward to the next stage. I had no idea then that the sport that had become my saviour would also be my downfall.

Chapter 7

THE SAINT

I went through some holdalls of old stuff at the weekend. They'd sat gathering cobwebs in Hephs' garage for years. Rummaging in the first one, my hand found a bit of ribbon. I pulled at it and out came my World Cup winners' medal. Digging a bit deeper I spotted something deep red. An England cap. The two biggest markers from my professional rugby career. I stared at them for a while and waited for some kind, any kind, of emotional response. I might as well have been staring at an ashtray and a flannel.

I found a Powergen Cup final shirt. Again, I stared hard, looked at the Northampton badge, felt the thick cotton in my hands. I turned to Hephs – 'I played in this game, did I?'

'Yes mate, of course you did. Against Gloucester, remember?' I didn't. Not just that game, any of them. The mental vault that contains my time at Saints has been invaded and picked clean by the illness. Incredible really. I made 195 appearances for Northampton, including a European Cup final, the club's first. Half the town travelled down to Twickenham to roar us on. I know – because I've read about it.

I went back to watch a game at Franklin's Gardens recently. I wondered if attending a match might jog some memories. It didn't – apart from two things. Straight away, the slope on the pitch made me recall how I preferred playing up the hill rather than down. And then there was the clock. I kept looking at it. There was something there. I knew there was a memory tied up with it, if only I could access it. The picture came in bits and pieces.

OK, so we're a few points down . . . it's near the end . . . the crowd is drifting away . . . they haven't realised the clock isn't how the referee times the game . . . and now there's shouting . . . they're running back in . . . we've scored really late on . . . we're winning . . . they want to see what the excitement is about.

I had it – a memory. A moment of triumph as big as any I'd experienced on this ground. But then I started thinking. *Why? Why that moment? Why the clock? Why was that specific moment suddenly dislodged from its place in the dying core of my brain when so many others refuse to budge?* That kind of randomness disturbs me. I'm reminded again of how out of sync with normality my brain is. Why would such an essentially pointless memory remain when so much else of true importance has been lost? It reminds me of when I was a kid. There was a toy called an Etch A Sketch. Everyone seemed to have one. You twiddled a couple of knobs and made a picture on the screen. Then you shook it and the picture disappeared, except sometimes you could still faintly see its outline. I think that's what's happened to my head. During my rugby career, it was constantly being shaken. Most of the pictures disappeared, but every now and then an outline was left. And that's what my brain uses now to build stories from the past.

If a picture has been completely erased, no outline left, then that's the end of it – gone. Ten years after the World Cup victory, for example, I played in a 'legends' game against the Aussies at the Twickenham Stoop. Somehow I managed to race – actually 'race' might be exaggerating it a bit – down the wing from deep in my own half to score an eighty-yard try. People were on their feet screaming as I made it to the line. I loved it – *Fantastic, there's something I've never done before.* But then a few days later I was chatting about it to a mate.

'Don't you remember?' he said. 'You did exactly the same for Saints in a Heineken Cup game against Glasgow in 2005.'

I have no recollection of that try, and can find no footage of it, but it's verified in a BBC match report, so must have happened. I'm sure if a recording does ever surface it will confirm me as a little less heavy than the 150 kilos of prime ex-pro that crashed over the line at the Stoop.

That charity game was the first time Steph had ever watched me play. She thought the try was great. It was too good an opportunity to miss. 'What, that?' I said nonchalantly. 'I used to do that all the time.'

In 1997, Saints paved the way for me to make rugby a full-time job by making me part of their new academy set-up, formed in recognition of the game's recently conferred professional status. That meant, for the first time, I was actually being paid. Not much – £200 a month plus my rent – but it's always a big moment for any sportsperson when finally they have that realisation – *Hang on! They're giving me money – to play a game?* To some degree, I'm not sure I ever left that thought behind. Throughout my career I came at contracts from a slightly different and more naïve angle than others whose parents might have been involved or who knew someone who could help them negotiate. Strangely, since I'd never seen much of it before rugby, I was never driven by money. The way I saw it then, and still do, is that there's always someone bigger and better than you, always someone earning more than you. On that basis, if I was happy with what I'd got I wouldn't go hunting for more. My attitude when a contract was put in front of me was simple – *What else am I going to do?* I wasn't exactly being bombarded with offers from outside the game. On its most basic level, my thoughts never veered from that initial: *I'm getting paid to play sport – this is brilliant!'*

Lodging with Mattie Stewart when I started at Saints, I'd lap it up as he told me stories about playing at international level, whetting my appetite massively to do the same. Mattie had high standards on and off the pitch. Ex-military, he wasn't far off ironing his cornflakes before pouring on the milk. Ben Cohen picked me up for training once and quickly made himself some toast before we cleared off. When I came back later, Mattie was steaming.

'Wally, this ain't working.'

'What do you mean?'

'The house is a state.'

I scanned round. It looked perfectly all right to me. Mattie took me into the kitchen and pointed. Ben's toast crumbs, still there on the worktop, were the offending items. Calmly, I brushed them into the palm of my hand and put them in the bin.

'I think we're all right again now, Mattie.'

I certainly had no issue keeping a pristine house. As a kid I'd get home from school and then have to scrub the place clean. Some might have rebelled against that and, once they'd left, never picked a brush up again. But I still love things to be neat and tidy. I've always looked good in a pair of Marigolds. Last Christmas I even treated myself to a new ironing board! I can't understand people who can't look after themselves. As someone who, thanks to dementia, faces being denied just that, it's even harder to understand. My own kids, young as they are, already cook with me. We all enjoy it and I know it will stand them in good stead for when they go their own way.

People would laugh but all I had possessions-wise at that time was a big pine bed and a mattress. I flitted between loads of different houses and flats and that bed was all that ever went with me. In some rooms it would fill the entire space. I'd open the door and slide beneath the duvet. That bed was one of my proudest purchases. Strange, really, because I was barely in it. I slept less than anyone I knew.

I was fortunate that, dismantled, my bed, with the boot open and possibly one of the doors, just about fitted in my new car – Hephs' nan's old Ford Fiesta. Despite it being nearly twenty years since this epic vehicle, cream on the outside, beige on the in, had rolled off the production line, it had just 20,000 miles on the clock. The old lady had used it just once a week to tootle up to the supermarket and back. Right from a kid I've always liked old cars – owning a Cortina and a Capri is my dream – and this was spotless, a mint condition example of an absolute classic. I wasn't to know it when I bought it, but that Fiesta would come into its own when the farmers and truckers blockaded the oil refineries during the fuel protests of 2000. With petrol at a premium, drivers queued for hours to get a meagre ration of diesel or unleaded. Except me that is. Being so old, the Fiesta still ran on four-star. I would whizz straight past dozens of fuming motorists to the forever empty four-star pump.

On one occasion, however, I was just screeching back on to the road when I saw blue lights behind me. My antics had attracted the attention of the local constabulary. I pulled in and two officers ambled over. They did a number plate check and it turned out the vehicle was untaxed. Nothing deliberate – I'd totally forgotten. One of them started taking the piss out of both me and the car and I gave him a friendly shove – well, what I consider a friendly shove. Next thing I knew he was on the floor. No way had I meant that to happen but I knew straight away I was in trouble.

'I'll get in the back of your car,' I offered as curtains started to twitch across the road.

'Oh, don't worry about him,' said the other officer. 'He's a bit soft. Just sort us out some tickets for the next home game.' I was still laughing about it as they drove away.

Away from rugby, Matt Bridge was putting a few quid in my pocket by offering me work for his construction company. Some of the other lads were also on the sites. It felt like, as a squad, we worked together, ate together and trained together. No wonder that, kicked out of my unhappy home, the set-up meant so much to me. I had been lacking a purpose in life and right there, with these mates, I had truly found it. This is what I mean when I tell people I never loved rugby as a sport. What I loved was the togetherness, the companionship, the feeling of belonging. I found even more of that when, as I began to progress towards the first team, Hephs' older brother, Saints fly half Ali, bought a house and I rented a room there with Hephs and scrum half Dom Malone. Putting a bunch of young rugby lads together in a house might sound like a recipe for mayhem, but actually we were clean, tidy and sometimes even quiet. The whole place was spotless. The kitchen was cleaned after every meal, although most nights we'd slump in a chair watching *Friends* while waiting for a pizza.

At that time, I was ridiculously full of energy. I'd be last to bed and first up in the morning. Day after day, Hephs would wake up to find me sat at the bottom of his bed staring at him, laughing. Eventually he banned me from his bedroom before nine in the morning, and later moved into an apartment with his partner. He did, however, make one supreme error. He was foolish enough to get a flat on the ground floor. At half seven in the morning, I'd be banging on his window – 'Hephs! Hephs! Are you coming out to play?'

◈

When eventually I started getting run-outs in Saints' midweek games, where young players were blooded, it was massive. And yet there was still frustration in me. I was two or three years younger than most of my peers and so would watch them progressing to the bigger games ahead of me. It left me feeling dejected, to the extent my attitude in training was suffering. One day, Tim Rodber, the sort of bloke who really knows if a player has what it takes to survive and achieve at the top level, called me over to the first-team training pitch. Without so much as a hello, he gave me a clump round the head. I didn't care who he was, how many England caps he had, how much power he held at the club, I wasn't having that off anyone. I went for him. He got hold of me before I could do any damage.

'I like that!' he said. He was just testing me out. He'd heard I was the up-and-coming lad, a bit edgy, and wanted to see what I was all about. From that point on he'd sit me down and make me understand what was required. Rodders knew how to make people feel confident about themselves. When I graduated into the first team proper, I'd watch as he'd go round the changing room pointing out the strength we had in there – 'Federico Méndez – the best front rower in the world! Garry Pagel – World Cup winner!' And then one day his gaze turned on me – 'Steve Thompson – you will play for England!' When a man like Tim Rodber says something like that, you sit up and listen.

If, however, someone had told me I'd play for England as hooker, I'd have replied that they most definitely needed their head looking at. It was Ian McGeechan who suggested I should shift from flanker to the front row. Initially I played at tighthead prop, but there was a growing feeling – same as would happen with England's coaches – that someone with my physical shape, allied to good handling skills and a decent turn of speed, was being wasted in a position where strength alone was key. Hooker, McGeechan concluded, was the place for me. In that position I would be unique. Most top-level hookers could do a half-decent job with the ball but were rarely compared to cheetahs when it came to speed. Yaks, yes. Cheetahs, no. Having played hooker a few times for East Midlands I wasn't a complete novice, but even so I wasn't expecting to make progress quite as quickly as I did. The weekend after McGeechan's brainwave I played for the development team in just that position. Barely had I got my head round that than I was selected for England Under-21s. Within two years I was pulling on the Number 2 shirt for England.

If that makes my transition from Saints' academy to England international appear about as bumpy as a bullet train, it's worth remembering not only my issue with lineouts, but also that I was most definitely Northampton's second-choice hooker behind the aforementioned Argentinian international Méndez. It got to the point where my head was turned by a northern lad I knew who told me I'd be perfect for rugby league. I got myself an agent, chosen with true professionalism on the basis he had a handlebar moustache, and the result was an approach from St Helens. That was it. I was ready to banish my lineout blues to history and drive north to sign on the dotted line. Except my car had other ideas. It resolutely refused to start. The meet-up with St Helens was postponed for a couple of days and in the intervening period Méndez got injured and I was promoted from the bench for Saints' game against London Irish. I did OK, scoring two tries and showing my turn of speed by catching their full back from behind. Not only that, but my lineout throws weren't half bad either. Union was back in the box seat. If the stars had aligned differently – if Méndez hadn't been injured or if I'd had a decent car – then this might be a very different story. World Cup, Lions, none of it would ever have happened.

I have no regrets over that decision. Yes, I'd have loved the freedom they have in league to run with the ball, and who knows where the game would have taken me? But in another way, I know the long-term result would have been exactly the same – a man in his forties finding out that, bit by bit, his brain is being stolen. The punishment players take in league is ridiculous, collision being an absolute fundamental of the game. Chances are I'd have ended up with even more brain damage than I have now. League is impact after impact, including training, and, sadly, there's no shortage of players from that format coming forward having been diagnosed with brain injuries and showing symptoms of dementia.

I expect I might also have felt like a bit of an alien in St Helens. Northampton was where my life was, somewhere I'd gone from being a nobody to a somebody. Because it's a rugby town, people think a lot of the club and by extension the players. The same of course goes for St Helens, but with Northampton there was a difference – I was a local lad. And whatever the sport, fans love nothing more than seeing a local lad do well. Those accolades, not big things but just someone giving me a pat on the back in the bar and saying, 'Well played, lad,' gave me a sense of belonging.

❖

It would be nice to give you chapter and verse on my time at Saints, but it isn't going to happen. If I can't remember a World Cup final then the chance of the nitty-gritty of individual Northampton matches suddenly popping up is thin. In fact, it was this very worry that made me so anxious about being inducted into the Premiership Rugby Hall of Fame in the summer of 2021.

Initially, I was struck with paranoia. *Maybe it's all bullshit. Maybe I wasn't any good. Maybe I've been asked because people feel a bit sorry for me.* It was totally nonsensical head chatter – I was actually asked before I was diagnosed. Then, when I saw that there was to be a Q&A element to the evening, the paranoia was replaced with dread. This was, after all, an occasion to celebrate my club achievements, and if my A to every Q was 'I haven't the foggiest' then it wasn't exactly going to add to the sparkle of the event. I felt more and more sick at the thought of getting up in front of people, to the extent that by the time the big day came round I felt as if I was travelling to an appointment with the guillotine. Of course, in the end everything was fine. I was inducted alongside two other Saints players, Grays and Christian Day, which made the conversational element a whole lot easier. I've got quite used to piggybacking on other people's memories. Someone will say, 'Remember when . . ?' and I'll say, 'Yeah!' and nod my head. Better to pretend than keep asking, 'What the hell are you on about?' and have them look at you like you're mad. I also know that my struggling to remember creates an atmosphere among other people, a nervousness on their part, and I don't want to be part of or the cause of that. My forgetfulness is not something about which I should ever feel embarrassed, but in certain circumstances if hiding it means less awkwardness for me and others, then it's something I'll do.

My surviving memories of my time at Saints are based almost entirely around my very early days at the club. I love catching up with the likes of Ali, Mattie, Dom and Hephs, because I can remember that era, albeit through a series of blurred images – like looking at a photo album while wearing someone else's glasses. I remember my first league game, for instance, against West Hartlepool, and how it felt for me, Hephs and the others who'd come through at the same time to receive our first-team ties. I also remember people such as former coach and director of rugby, John Steele. An ex-army officer, John took no prisoners, but somehow we clicked. He talked to me like a grown-up, gave me direction on and off the pitch, and was an incredible source of advice and inspiration. Such memories leave me with a good feeling – one so lacking when I try to slot myself back into other times of my career. Do that and it's not so much a good feeling as no feeling at all. Without memory, there can be no sense of belonging. There are no mileposts, no markers, nothing familiar to cling on to. At that point I am floundering, clutching at anything. I am lost and empty.

Sometimes it feels like early days memories, my childhood in Northampton, for example, and my first few years in rugby, are being cleaned up and polished while the later stuff is being hauled out of my head by a bunch of clumsy removal men and thrown in a van. Armed with the information I now have about brain injury there's an obvious reason why my memory peters out so early. From that point on, my head, like the rest of me, started taking a relentless and daily battering. The jigsaw was upended. Half the pieces went up the vacuum and the rest were just blue sky.

It helped massively to talk to Dawn Astle, daughter of legendary West Brom striker Jeff Astle who developed dementia from heading footballs during his career and died from CTE aged just fifty-nine in 2002. After a long family campaign, a study commissioned by the Football Association and the Professional Footballers' Association found that ex-footballers are around three and a half times more likely to die from dementia than the general population. Unloading on to someone who understands always helps, and Dawn, whose family set up the Jeff Astle Foundation to raise awareness of brain injury in all forms of sport and offer much needed support to those affected, showed me an image of what experts call the dementia 'bookcase'. In good health, the graphic shows we have shelves full of memories, older towards the bottom, newer at the top. Over time, the higher shelves thin out to nothing as dementia steals our short-term memory. The shelves below also start to empty but hold on to some volumes, with the bottom shelf retaining the most. As someone with early-onset dementia, I could have been frightened witless by that image – pages and pages of stories and information tumbling from those shelves never to be replaced – but actually I thanked Dawn for showing me, because for once my illness made perfect sense. I thought about how difficult I find it to remember something from five minutes ago while still being able to summon up a perfect memory of playing in the street as a kid – how those early memories feel clear and clean while other points of my life are covered in a thick layer of dust. On a practical level, it helped me to understand my present and my future. My bottom shelf is still looking good, but those above will come to have more and more space. When a book is taken from those shelves it's not going to be put back. As it stands, the book about those very early years at Northampton is losing a few pages but is otherwise generally intact.

Occasionally, though, the loss of a volume is particularly poignant. There were times when, like a lot of players, I visited sick children in hospital. Over time, relationships with families would develop and become significant. I took one child's favourite toy, a cuddly seal I think, with me on that 2005 Lions tour to help raise awareness of his illness. Another time I helped organise a box at the Saints for a lad who, awfully, didn't have long to live. It was something for him to look forward to at least. I feel dreadful that I can't remember more about such incredible people. Again, I feel disrespectful. How could I forget? How could anyone forget? And that's the thing – yes, I can't remember the high points of my career, but, when you think about it, that's nothing compared to the things in life that really matter.

If I'm to stay positive, I know I cannot keep beating myself up over my inability to remember important elements of my life. To allow myself to move forward, I have to accept they've vanished from my head. Guilt, the fight to remember, and the inevitable feeling of failure when that doesn't happen, is too big a drain on the ever-diminishing battery pack I have left. It's hard and, to me at least, it's selfish, but sometimes I have to allow memories, clinging on by their fingernails, to fall away to their deaths. After all, once they've gone, the guilt will go – I'll never know they, or it, existed.

Chapter 8

GRENADE

It's hard living in a half-world where memories either stutter to a halt or slam straight into a brick wall, but what confuses me more than anything about Saints is how and why I left, walking out on a four-year contract to sign for Brive. I'd never shown any interest in living in France, didn't know anyone there, didn't speak the language, and didn't even particularly like the French. And yet I voluntarily left my refuge, the surrogate family that was Northampton Saints, and, by heading into the complete unknown, sought out the exact opposite. It's as if I flipped. Northampton was everything to me. If they'd told me to play on one leg, I would have done it. They were my life, my saviour. Northampton was more than a club, a place to play sport: it was somewhere that propped me up as a person. The more I look back on such flashpoints in my life, the more I feel so many of them came from grenades manufactured on the factory floor of head injury. The more convinced I am that the damage to my brain would have been causing erratic behaviour way back into my twenties.

Talking to staff and players, they tell me my mindset at the time was that the club had turned its back on me. While I'd painted a picture in my head of myself at Northampton forever, in the end I'd concluded that the relationship mattered more to me than it did to them, annoyed that players with no attachment to the club were being brought in at the expense of home-grown talent. We'd won the European Cup in 2000 with a massive contingent of local lads. For me, the thing to have done then was to build on that success with a few new players, but the club went way too far in that direction, buying in so many new faces. Not only that, but those players were being given preferential treatment, handed their club cap when still below what had always been the required number of appearances. To succeed in rugby at any level, togetherness is key. Look at teams like Leicester, Northampton and Exeter, and at their best they've always had a core of local boys, built upon with great players from elsewhere. And yet still teams go down the wrong road. You might buy a championship team, but you won't build a legacy. What you'll actually get is robots; 3D printouts of what's needed in any position.

There's a lot of falsehoods around professional sport. In rugby, there's this idea that a group of players is tight; that if the shit hits the fan on or off the pitch, they'll all be there for each other. Truth is, I've seen that happen, but only when playing in teams where we'd all come through together, knew each other and looked after one another. That unity massively helped the team. It gave us an extra edge. If a player wasn't the best but was someone we trusted, someone we knew would give everything, then the rest of us would raise our game to help them out and make sure they stayed in the team. In a physical game, playing for one another brings so much. But as the game got more and more professional, teams less and less closely bound, I would increasingly see players whose first priority was their pay packet.

It's hard when you see a team that means so much to you head in a different direction. From the outside you can maybe take a more measured view, but when you're in it you can't help but be consumed by what's going on. I know things like that would have upset me. I have always felt that in a team, everyone should be treated the same or else the entire ethos is undermined. In the black-and-white world of my bruised and battered head, a violation of those standards would have been a definite flashpoint. Maybe I was naïve in seeing my relationship with Saints as being beyond a business transaction, but even so why turn my whole life upside down? Why hack away at my safety net? Grays, coach at the time, says he'd talked to me about building a team around me and felt he'd persuaded me to stay. I was about to agree to do just that when club chairman Keith Barwell came into the room and told me bluntly that I had a contract and should honour it. The mood of optimism and positivity that Grays had so carefully nurtured was punctured and that was it, no going back. But even if leaving Northampton was a must, going to Brive remains a puzzle. I was still at my peak in 2007. I expect there would have been plenty of English clubs more than happy to take me. I could have made it all so much easier. Instead, something just snapped and I isolated myself further by going abroad.

Now I know how CTE can cause drastic personality changes, I find the move easier to understand. I see that 2007 explosion for what it was, the first of several which came either around the time of a significant concussion or as a result of the worsening condition of my brain. In fact, in assessing signs of CTE, these are the exact pointers, the big behavioural swerves, that experts now ask people to look out for. Those close to me have told me my personality changed during those later years at Northampton. But I wasn't looking out for anything. I had no idea I was behaving irrationally or oddly. I was just being me. In my head, it was the people around me, or situations, that were causing me problems. And because of that I left Northampton, the town that had been, through thick and thin, my home, and instead became a nomad.

◈

The Brive deal was sealed in the most incredible hotel in Paris. Everything was gilded. Even the toilet seats were worth more than my house. My delegation consisted of an agent and Hephs. The Brive delegation was a little more refined, made up of club chairman Simon Gillham and various officials representing the billionaire owner and French entrepreneur Daniel Derichebourg. Brive had won the Heineken Cup in the nineties but were now struggling, with a real possibility of dropping out of France's top division. They were looking to rebuild, to become a real presence, and I would be their first big signing as they entered this new era. They were impressed when I said I'd sign regardless of whether they were relegated so long as they remained ambitious and would still put money into the club. They liked that commitment and we shook on the deal. I would see out the rest of the season at Northampton and head over to France.

And then I broke my neck.

It was a Heineken Cup match against Biarritz. I was tackled in an odd judo-type move which swung me round and slammed me headfirst into the ground. The immediate result was a loss of movement in my right arm. I played on for a while but it was obvious this wasn't something that was just going to sort itself out. The physio could see I was in trouble and so I was taken off. Tests revealed a prolapsed cervical disc. In layman's terms, the shock-absorbing bit separating the vertebrae had been forced against my spinal cord. Surgery was the only option.

After the op, Hephs came to visit me in hospital and, believing me to be seriously incapacitated, was soon spooning soup and dropping grapes into my mouth. It was like being a high-ranking Roman, with Hephs as my personal slave. While he was there, a couple of Bath players I knew walked in with a pizza. Like a shot, I sat bolt upright and grabbed a slice. Witnessing this miracle-like recovery, Hephs was, for some reason, not a happy bunny.

I'd initially hoped I might be able to play after a few months' rest. But I was advised the injury was a career-ender. To carry on, I was told, would be reckless and leave me open to long-term, potentially permanent, spinal damage. I announced my retirement and England coach Brian Ashton was first on the phone. He expressed his condolences and told me I'd always be welcome in the England camp. When he said that, I don't think he, me or anyone else, expected my eventual return to be in full England regalia.

Naturally, I thought that was it for me and Brive. They were investing in a World Cup-winning hooker, not what I'd effectively become – an ex-pro with a broken neck. I couldn't have been more wrong. 'You were going to be loyal to us,' they told me, 'so we'll be loyal to you.' I would go to Brive not as a player but as a coach.

In all honesty, there was a significant part of me that was actually relieved when I was told it was all over and I would never be pulling the boots on in anger again. Rugby-wise, I was blown. It was more than just physical exhaustion: constant playing meant my spirit had been worn down too. Unlike me, it seemed like every other England player in that 2003 World Cup squad had gone through an enforced period on the sidelines due to injury at one time or another. No one wants to be twiddling their thumbs for months on end, but that gap does allow a player to mentally reset, renew ambition and rebuild desire. Others had chosen to use the tournament as their swansong. Going out on a high is every sportsperson's dream, but it very rarely happens. Like me, they carry on until what was once the thing that they lived for becomes first the everyday, and then, at its worst, when burnout hits, a treadmill. Performance levels drop and you slip lower and lower down the ranks. Cheery, it isn't. Even less so when you come to realise that your brain has been smashed to bits along the way.

By the time the neck injury happened, no two ways about it, I was mentally shot. Somewhere in the mud of Franklin's Gardens I'd lost my love of the game. Call it my mojo, call it what you want, but my passion for rugby was non-existent. It reminded me a little of the listlessness I'd felt after the World Cup. I'd worked so hard to achieve the biggest accolade in the sport, and then suddenly it was, 'OK, is that it?' It took me back to being a kid, waking up on Boxing Day after the excitement of Christmas. You think that feeling – the build-up and the day itself – is going to last forever, but then inevitably it slides into something much more mundane and familiar. For some of the lads, that World Cup was a defining feature of their life map. They would now either carry on playing through the next World Cup cycle or retire. I'd never seen the game as a journey, a road I was destined always to travel. I hadn't gone searching for success. Rugby had come into my life. It was something that just happened to me.

At Saints, it had reached the point where I was a heartbeat away from quitting the game and fulfilling my childhood ambition of joining the police. With my real dad being a copper, the connection was in the family, but the idea was based on more solid ground than just that. In Northampton a lot of my friends were coppers and so they'd arrange for me to go out on the streets with them. Kitted up in a stab vest and all the gear, I absolutely loved seeing the sharp end of the job and had massive respect for the officers out there in the thick of it. I would even sometimes get involved, reasoning with the odd group of likely-looking lads potentially up to no good. Because of my background I felt I was good at using language they understood. Speak to people on their terms and they respond. The minute you're aloof, the barrier goes up.

That whole idea of service appealed to me so much that my rugby career very nearly didn't happen at all. On a few occasions as a teenager, I was tempted to venture into the Army Recruitment Centre in Northampton. Unsurprising then that when, in my England days, I was asked to go out to Camp Bastion in Afghanistan for the opening of a new hospital wing, I jumped at the chance. I had incredible admiration for the work the soldiers were doing there and was amazed I might be able to see it first-hand. Right from the minute the transport plane touched down, the scale of the operation blew me away. Out of blank, featureless desert, an operational site the size of Reading had been created. One day the soldiers took me and my companion, my old England colleague Neil Back, out of the compound in an armoured vehicle. There were three gates we could leave by. As we went through one, a bomb went off at another. The soldiers in our vehicle barely reacted. It struck me how what they considered routine was so far removed from anything the rest of us could ever experience.

We crawled through the streets of a neighbouring town and I watched through thick glass as little kids smiled and waved while their parents spat on the floor in disgust. I turned my head to the windscreen and again and again saw cars screaming towards us. Were they going to attack? Or was it just that on the roads of this place there were no rules? I couldn't get over how this was the everyday for these soldiers. The constant danger and anxiety. Time and again, they would make a rugby analogy – the strategy, the working together, the need for unity. I could see what they were saying but at the same time I'd interrupt: 'It's OK, you really don't have to try and make it fit. The worst thing that can happen to us is losing a game. You could lose a limb, or worse.'

It amazed me how humble everyone was, talking down the incredible job they were doing, the fact they were risking their lives. We met one young lad at the hospital who'd been injured in an explosion that killed his mate. The nursing staff told us he'd barely spoken since the incident. Backy and I sat down, not expecting much more than a nod of the head and a hello. We couldn't believe it when straight away he offloaded to us about what had happened and how he couldn't wait to get back to his family. He must have somehow felt comfortable with us; it was an incredible moment and one which delivered a hell of a lot of perspective on life, perspective that I still dwell on now. My issue comes from playing a game. Soldiers' issues come from fighting a war.

We were also taken to see the work of the team in charge of the dogs that chase down suspects and sniff out explosives. They told us they'd started working with a new breed, not much bigger than a springer spaniel, and asked if one of us fancied being padded up while it gave chase. I've had dogs, big ones, Great Danes and the like, and know how strong they are. I really didn't fancy being pursued and mauled to the ground by one. Backy, though, was bang up for it – I put it down to small-man syndrome (he's not the tallest bloke) – and disappeared to put on the protective suit. Ten minutes later he returned looking like he was about to play goalkeeper in an ice hockey match.

'When I shout "Go!",' said the officer, 'I want you to start running.'

A couple of army lads pointed at a high wall. 'Get up there,' they told me. 'You don't want to be in the way.'

They hauled me up just as the beast was released. 'Go!' the officer bellowed and, slavering at the mouth and with the acceleration of a Ferrari, what appeared to be a small bear thundered past. I couldn't see Backy behind his mask but was fairly sure his expression was one of blind terror as he looked over his shoulder and saw this ball of froth and fur heading straight for him. In terms of a fair contest it was like pitching an ageing tortoise against Usain Bolt. Within seconds, the dog smashed into Backy with such force that it looked for all the world like his spine was going to snap. It was all over him, snarling, dragging him round, biting into and puncturing the suit, spilling drool through the mask and on to his face. Even the handler was having trouble getting it to stop.

I looked at the blokes alongside me on the wall. 'Quite a bit bigger than a springer spaniel,' I noted. Backy staggered to his feet, looking like he'd gone five rounds with Mike Tyson. I was happy I'd made the right call.

The army was never going to happen once I'd started playing rugby, but a massive part of me wishes I'd stepped away from the game when I'd had a chance. Quitting after the neck injury would have spared my brain a second onslaught of impacts and concussions. Of course, I wasn't to know that at the time and so, catastrophically, I set out on a road which would eventually lead straight back to the exact same hospital bed.

Chapter 9

LOST IN FRANCE

Most players would take a flight over to France. I had other plans, involving a motorbike. I'd tried to get my licence when I was at Northampton but John Steele wouldn't let me.

'You can't stop me,' I told him. 'It's not in my contract.'

'It is now,' he said, and wrote it in beneath my signature. To be fair to John, he was just looking out for me. 'Out of all the people in this squad,' he explained, 'you are not getting a motorbike. You are fearless.'

But when Brive took me on, the shackles were off and I seized my chance. I bought a brand new 1100cc Triumph Speed Triple, and then, at the crack of dawn, set off to bike the 750 miles from Northampton. In the Eurotunnel I found myself surrounded by hardcore bikers heading for a weekend at the German motorcycle Grand Prix. They were full of admiration for my machine.

'How long have you been riding?'

'I looked at my watch. Well, about eight . . . '

'Eight years! You don't look old enough!'

'No, eight hours. I'm heading to Brive, just north of Toulouse.'

'Oh. OK. How long will that take? Two or three days – enjoy the roads, take in the sights?'

'No, I'll be there this evening.'

I could see them rolling their eyes as they walked away. In a matter of seconds, I'd gone from the cool kid with the amazing motorbike to the idiot with the new toy.

At least when I got there the club couldn't have been more welcoming, Simon Gillham particularly so, doing his best to make me feel part of his lovely family. The 2007 World Cup was predominantly held in France that autumn and alongside Simon I watched England's winning semi-final against the hosts from a corporate box at the Stade de France. Great, were it not for the fact that the box was full of extremely passionate and patriotic French supporters. 'Don't cheer!' Simon kept telling me as England forced their way to victory. I did my best, honest.

Naturally, with a broken neck, I'd been looking forward to a rather less full-on World Cup experience in 2007. But then, as part of the opening ceremony, I discovered I'd been chosen to do my least favourite thing – throw a lineout. *What? Really? I thought I'd been invited along for a bit of a day out!* There's another thing I remember from that day – how mad it seemed that I'd been asked. *Why me? I don't deserve this.* I knew I was part of the team that had won the tournament last time round, hence the request, but that was how my mind always worked. With that particular torture out of the way, I settled in to watch the tournament from the comfort of various bars – and corporate boxes – around Paris.

I was incredibly grateful for Simon's generosity in taking me under his wing. Retiring is hard enough at the best of times without it happening overnight at a time when you're still at the peak of your career. I had effectively found myself in a foreign country, on my own, with the entire reason for me being there taken away by circumstances beyond my control. Without the comfort blanket of the game, I felt lost, isolated and, a lot of the time, confused. Simon has since said he saw a fragility and vulnerability in me at that time. He recalls instances where he'd look at me and find me staring blankly into mid-air. He'd ask me if I was OK, and I'd say I was, but I really wasn't. I was living under a dark cloud, thinking, *What have I done?* I'd left all my touchstones behind and literally just headed off somewhere I knew no one and didn't speak a word of the language. I'd gone from having familiarity, security and a successful career to suddenly being hundreds of miles distant from any of it. I felt hopelessly lost. So much had happened in such a short period that I just didn't have the headspace to deal with it. My brain – my ill brain – couldn't make sense of what was going on. The routes it had usually found out of a difficult situation had been cut off. Rugby had always been my salvation, and in a split second it had gone.

The only thing that gave me some kind of escape from this overwhelming feeling of doom was my new home's passion for wild-boar hunting. I'd always liked country sports and soon took it up myself. But that meant keeping a shotgun. Looking back now, it scares me. I lived on my own and on one occasion found myself sat on my bed, head in hands, crying, the gun just a few feet away. I could see it out of the corner of my eye. It would have taken zero effort to reach across and take it in my hands. I imagined myself pointing it at my head and pulling the trigger. There was only one thing that stopped me doing just that – I kept the cartridges downstairs. Had that not been the case, this story would I'm sure have ended right there. As it was, that little bit of separation was enough to provide the physical jolt that saved me.

I recognised enough about my emotions to see I was massively lost in retirement. I was only in my twenties. I was struggling now, so what was the rest of it going to be like? If I was going to survive, I had to do something drastic. That's when the seed was sown: *Maybe I can play again.*

Specialists took a look at my neck and felt the repair had settled so well that there was nothing to stop me making a return. In fact, if anything, my neck was stronger than when the injury happened. I had 90 per cent movement, compared to less than half that before. I felt that, if all went well, I had five years or more rugby left in me. I vowed I wouldn't aim low. I would try to reclaim my spot in the England side. But it wasn't the thought of more glory that inspired my fight, nor was it financial reward. I had injured my neck after forty-seven caps. More than anything I wanted to get to fifty so Keith Picton could keep his pledge and finally see me in an England shirt. Keith gave me so much but never asked for anything back. I wanted at least to give him that.

If, back then, re-entering the sport looked like a saviour from the bullet, I sometimes now wonder if I was actually just killing myself in a different way. After all, had I not put my head through four further years of punishment, maybe my diagnosis might not have been so bleak. Then again, I'd played a lot of rugby by 2007, so who knows? What I fervently do believe is that stopping playing for a year gave my brain a chance to recharge, to consume the world around it without constant violent impacts being rained down on it, which is why, compared to the years previous at Northampton, there are elements of my time at Brive I remember quite well. I know, for instance, that playing for Brive never meant as much to me as playing for Northampton. When I was captain of Saints, I would sometimes really go at it in the changing room – shouting, swearing – because the club was in my bones and its success was everything to me. At Brive, I could never quite find that fire, although my three years there still mean an awful lot to me.

My new employers were brilliant with my comeback. Obviously, the club could see that if it came off they would finally end up with the player they'd signed a year or so previously. But there was some significant work to be done before that could be the case. Off the pitch, I would have to give back the half-million-pound insurance pay-out I'd received after breaking my neck. On the pitch, I would have to be more determined than ever. Getting injured was the first time in a long time I'd escaped being bound to a certain weight and so I'd really tucked into my food and drink. With my body so tired, relaxing, doing what I wanted, didn't seem a bad thing to do. The result was I heaped on the fat, at one stage reaching 150 kilos – 30 kilos heavier than my playing weight. I went from 18 stone of proper unit to 23 stone of blancmange. Remarkably, it was at this point I did a 700-mile bike ride from Greenwich to Mont Blanc in the Alps to raise money for the Bobby Moore Fund for Cancer Research. It seemed a good opportunity to get a few kilos off while raising a bit of money for a good cause. Although I did no training, I managed, so the engine was obviously still there. Typically, though, other than a climb on the last day, when the rest of the riders gave me an award for being slowest on the bike without falling off, I can't remember a turn of the wheel. The ride exists in my brain only as a warm glow.

However, the bike ride couldn't hide the stark truth of my physical condition. Playing at 150 kilos was a physical impossibility and so Brive brought in Bernard, a fitness coach on short-term loan from hell. Bernard absolutely beasted me. At our first session, I collapsed on the floor, gasping for breath and vomiting. Seeing this spewing lump at his feet, his view was simple – there was no way I'd be able to get myself back to playing fitness, to be a 'rugby man', as the French put it. His words were a red rag to a bull. I was determined to show him he was wrong, to change his mind completely. From that moment I dug in. I invested everything I had in his plan, and in so doing I won his respect. For six weeks I did nothing but train. The rest of the players would be off home and I'd still be out there, running, getting fit, getting back to game pace. Given a goal, I have always been incredibly focused with training; in it completely, almost obsessive–compulsive. One day, Simon was visited by a friend who wanted to invest in the club but felt professional sportspeople were pampered and overpaid. He then went out to have a look at the training facilities only to be presented with the sight of me so exhausted that I was literally throwing up down myself as I ran along. I don't know whether he invested. What I do know is I lost 25 kilos in six weeks. Thanks to Bernard, ten months after I hobbled off the pitch against Biarritz, I was back in the front row. I did, however, have one almighty scare. In a training session, my head slammed into an opposition player's chest. The compression on my neck felt horribly similar to the one that had 'ended' my career. Initially, I thought my return was over before it had begun. Then I realised one big difference from the previous injury – this time I could feel my arm. I was going to be OK. Knowing I could play at 100 per cent was massive to me. You can't play hooker and be holding something back. It's a position that's all or nothing. I needed to trust my body to give me that. I needed top-level rugby. In periods of self-contemplation, I was still capable of feeling very down, but the relentless demands of professional sport gave me a purpose. In reality, of course, I know now I was just papering over some very big cracks.

◈

I loved playing in France but got the feeling that French players really didn't love me back. I'm not sure exactly what gave me that impression, but it might have been something to do with the number of punches thrown at me in games – and how the French referees did absolutely nothing about it. Eventually, I asked one of the French contingent at Brive what was going on.

'Look,' he told me, 'it's not just the players; no one really likes you in France.'

'Oh, right,' I said, a bit taken aback.

'It's the way you used to sing the national anthem,' he continued. 'You looked so arrogant.'

Well, pardon me for breathing.

To be fair to the French, it's not just them who saw how I was on the pitch and thought I was exactly the same off it. The amount of times I had people say to me, 'Oh, actually, you're a really nice bloke, aren't you? Quiet and down to earth.' I don't know what they expected – maybe I was supposed to run at them, drag them to the floor and sit on them. Having said that, I encountered more than a few players who were as big a knob off the pitch as they were on it.

Above left: About as fresh-faced as you could possibly get. Or, as I could possibly get. © *Getty Images / David Rogers*

Above right: I was a style icon off the pitch long before David Beckham started strutting around in sarongs and slippers.

© *Getty Images / Phil Cole*

Middle: Brutal gym sessions quickly became part of my life training in the professional ranks.

© *Getty Images / David Rogers*

Left: …as did the repetitive impacts of the scrum machine. A ton-weight of men hurling themselves head-first at a massive iron tank.

© *Getty Images / David Rogers*

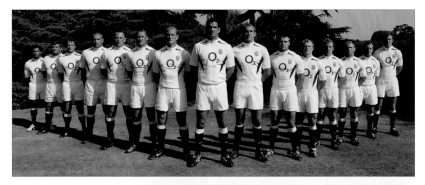

Above: Lining up alongside my England teammates in the build-up to the World Cup final. It sounds mad to say I look at these photos and I can't remember any of it. But I can't.

© *Getty Images / David Rogers*

Middle: Believe it or not, I used to be quick for a big lump. I used to beat people on the field with skill, before the game became about being a battering ram.

© *Getty Images / Mark Nolan*

Below: Preparing to lock into a scrum in the heat of the final. I'd change it all now and undo the damage if I could. © *Getty Images / Bob Thomas*

Above left: Things got crazy in the build up to the final. Here I am, with Martin Johnson, beamed up on the side of a skyscraper over Sydney harbour. © *Getty Images / Daniel Berehulak*

Above right: What a mug! Hitting the obligatory World-Cup-trophy-on-head pose during our victory parade. © *Getty Images / David Rogers*

Below: Celebrating winning the Rugby World Cup with my teammates, spraying champagne around, should be one of the happiest memories of my life. But I don't have it – there's nothing there when I go looking. © *Getty Images / Odd Andersen*

Above: I can't remember what Clive and I were laughing at here, at the England Legends vs Australia Legends game in 2013… but it was probably to do with a twenty-stone lump like me skinning two players and pelting 80 meters up the pitch to score a try (*inset*). Like I said, used to do it all the time!

© *Getty Images / Tom Shaw - RFU*

Below: At Twickenham, being inducted into the Premiership Rugby Hall of Fame in 2021. © *Getty Images / Ben Hoskins*

Above: My old pals, Lewis Moody and Ben Cohen (believe it or not, in his pants again). Mates on the pitch all those years ago and, I'm glad to say, still mates off it today. Legends, the pair of them. *(© Getty Images / David Rogers / Damien Meyer)*

Below: My Steph. We're not always dressed like this, I promise.

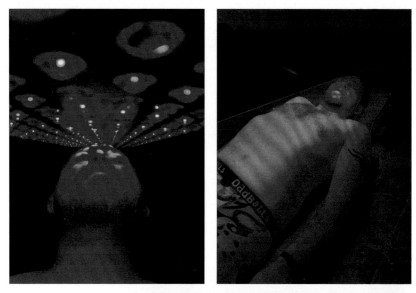

Above: I do a lot to counteract the effects of my dementia, and this red-light therapy is incredible for you in all sorts of ways, dementia or not. Looks mad though!

Middle: In the car with my family, my kids, my world.

Left: Cheers at Christmas!

Below: I love fishing on the Manchester shipping canal and other places. I have some dark moments there, but it's one of the good things in life.

Above: Still a dab-hand in the kitchen, and I make a killer roast. Here's a proper tip from me to you: do your pork crackling over with a hair dryer. Trust me!

Left: I love working outdoors – never did mind getting my hands dirty. But dementia is slowly robbing me even of my ability to do that.

Above/below: But I can still carry my beautiful kids on my shoulders, and sit them on my lap. That won't be changing for a long time.

Above/below left: No matter what the road ahead holds, I'll always try and be Superman for my wife and, most of all, for my kids.

Right: Seren, Slone, Saskia and Saxon. Everything I do is for you now. Love you all. (Bonus points if you spotted the dog!)

In France, the rugby was tough. The off-the-ball stuff was especially horrendous, and the French players understood exactly how to get away with it. They had worked out that in a televised game, the cameras would stay on a ruck for three seconds. You would actually hear them count – 'Un, deux, trois' – and then the moment they got to 'quatre' – bang! – they'd punch you in the face. They were also the worst for grabbing your bollocks and gouging your eyes. After a game against a French side, the skin around my eyes would often be red raw. As a rugby player, you don't stand on someone's head, you don't gouge and you don't grab the bollocks. But the French never seemed to accept any of that. They loved the old bollock-grabbing in particular. They'd give them a proper good twist. Agony. Absolute agony. At Brive, the other hooker in the squad revealed he wore a cricket box – 'You'll soon know why.' As an outsider, I felt that some French players made a thing about being hard when actually what they were doing was plain cowardice. If a French side tried that sort of stuff when I was playing for an English club, we'd make sure we gave them a good hiding.

Generally, I got on OK with the French lads at Brive, although there were occasional ups and downs. At one point, the players, as a group, agreed we wanted to get rid of the coaching team. When he got wind of the mutiny, the head coach came over screaming and shouting. Immediately, the French lads grouped together. 'It's not us,' they told him, pointing in the direction of the small English contingent. 'It's them who want you out.'

I like my history – maybe it makes up for forgetting my own – and once or twice I tried to have a chat with French teammates about the war. I was genuinely interested to hear what French people think about that period of time. It was like it never happened. Instead, they'd talk about ancient battles in which they'd come out on top over the English. The rest of it simply wasn't up for discussion. France is a beautiful country – I honestly do love it there – but it really did feel as if we English were public enemy number one. I remember once I was sat outside a coffee bar chatting to a mate and a bloke crossing the road tripped on the kerbstone.

'Fucking English!' he muttered and continued on his way.

Aside from the abuse (actually, most French people couldn't be friendlier), I really admired how the French lived their lives. They didn't max out on credit cards filling their homes full of crap – big tellies and the like. They lived well within their means so they could use that extra money for something that would really make them happy, a holiday home perhaps, or a get-together with family and friends. If a French person invited you round to their house, it wasn't to show you their flash new motor – chances are their car would be all battered up in the drive – it was to show you some real friendship and great hospitality. They had a very pragmatic attitude to life, even leaving their handbrake off when parking so another driver could shove their car up a few inches to get into a space. I really loved how relaxed they made everything, how much pressure they took off themselves. It's something I think about now as I try to take the stress out of my own life.

With the comeback going well and no sign of any issues with my old neck injury, a few months later I rang Martin Johnson, then England team manager, to say I was looking to get my place back. His reaction wasn't quite what I'd envisaged – he could barely breathe he was laughing that much – but actually it made perfect sense. I thought back to when Johnno had last seen me, at the opening ceremony of the World Cup in 2007, when I was a complete mess.

We met for dinner, which was when he saw the weight I'd lost, and the effort I'd made to turn myself back into an elite player and recapture my love of the game. Others, though, looked for motives elsewhere. Early on in the process, I overhead a member of the England coaching staff say they thought I was only doing it for the money. Inevitable I suppose – some people always think the worst – but it seriously pissed me off and I was glad when I forced him to swallow his words. My performances at Brive, the passion and determination I showed, made his accusations look petty-minded and silly, which is precisely what they were.

Within eighteen months of stepping back on to the rugby pitch, I got my England place back. A 16-9 victory over Argentina in November 2009 was my fiftieth cap and, with Keith, as promised, there in the stand, the most pleasurable of my career. The meeting of past and present, professional and personal. The culmination of so much.

Look carefully at pictures of that fiftieth cap and you'll see I'm wearing boots held together with tape. I would give away so much kit but just couldn't let boots go. I once watched

Jason Robinson change from one pair of new boots into another at half-time, not because there was anything wrong with the ones he was wearing but because he could. I could never do that. I had boxes of new boots ready and waiting, but I always wore boots out because it was what I was used to. For me, you had to wear them until they were dead. It didn't make sense not to.

◈

Having worked so hard to get back into the team, the World Cup in New Zealand in 2011 turned out to be nothing short of a disaster. Because of our outside centre Mike Tindall's recent marriage to Zara Phillips, the press attention on the off-field stuff was fiercer than anything I'd ever known, coming to a head with an infamous night out at the Altitude bar in Queenstown. Mid-World Cup, it's traditional to have a little blowout. It alleviates the pressure on the squad and presses the reset button. On this occasion, the blowout coincided with what the bar was advertising as a 'Mad Midget Weekender'. This entailed, as some newspapers put it, several 'dwarves' being thrown. I'll put my hand up right now and admit I was part of this spur-of-the-moment and highly regrettable escapade. When I got back to the hotel, I sent some suitably incriminating pictures to Hephs back in England. I woke up the next morning to find his reply. 'You didn't need to send pictures. The whole thing's all over the papers.' *Shit!* While we should never have behaved in the way we did, to some degree we felt we'd been a bit stitched up. The Irish boys had been in Altitude the week before doing the same thing – one of the 'dwarves' still had Ireland flags drawn on his face – but they didn't get any of the stick that we did.

From then on it was open season. At one point, I took a motorbike trip round the coast from Dunedin – a great way of getting away from the mix. Former England hooker Brian Moore hired a bike from the same place, heard I'd been in and proceeded to write a highly critical column for the *Daily Telegraph* describing my trip as 'madness'. It annoyed me – he had no idea why I'd done it or what I'd gained from it. He'd just waded in with his own blinkered view and that was that. To me, it felt like he was jumping on the bandwagon. We were there to be knocked down and he was quite happy to grab the nearest sledgehammer.

On the pitch, we didn't fare much better. While that year we'd had a good series in Australia and also won the Six Nations, in the World Cup we massively failed to fulfil our potential and lost to an average French team in the quarter-final. We had the opportunity to do something special and as a group we didn't take it.

The entire trip was forgettable in every sense. In fact, what shocks me most now as I look back is an interview I did with *The Observer* before we flew out to the tournament. As you'd expect, the journalist asked for my memories of the final in 2003. Given what I know now, my reply is shocking. 'I seriously can't remember it,' I tell the reporter. 'Things happened so quickly. There's bits and bobs, like walking out on the pitch before the match or going with the lads for coffee, but the actual game, nothing.' At the time I attribute 'this amnesia', as the journalist puts it, to a hundred-miles-an-hour lifestyle. It never occurred to me that my brain might have been addled by a decade and more of impact injuries. That answer really was an indicator of a deeper decline to come.

Chapter 10

SHUTDOWN

There was pretty much only one highlight from the World Cup in 2011 – Steph. She was a promotions girl with Emirates Airlines, one of the main tournament sponsors. We'd been knocked out by France and, being a bit down, I'd taken a sleeping tablet. I fancied switching off and then the next day would head over to Waiheke Island with a couple of the lads for a bit of wine-tasting, away from the rugby bubble.

It was nearing midnight when my roommate came back and woke me while getting amorous with his girlfriend. I couldn't lie there listening to that and so got up and went down to the bar.

'We're just about to close,' the waiter told me.

'No problem,' I said, 'give me five bottles of red.' With stash in hand, I sat in a corner drinking by myself until

England forwards coach Graham Rowntree spotted me and came over. There were a couple of good-looking girls in the bar as well who I assumed were Russian prostitutes. This might seem like a total generalisation, but the Russians were competing at that World Cup and had actually arrived in town with a few ladies of the night.

The girls came over, and I was waiting to be propositioned when one of them opened her mouth. Out came a Scouse accent. I got over that quickly enough and soon we were having a great laugh. She told us she'd been in one of the boxes at the game and asked whereabouts we'd been at the ground.

'The green bit,' Graham replied.

'Oh, where's that?' she asked, confused.

We arranged to meet back in the bar the following night, a date I nearly missed because the return trip from the wine-tasting almost ended in disaster. We'd had a really good afternoon and were chilling on the boat back when we started having one of those daft conversations. You know how when you're on a balcony of a high building and the next balcony is fifteen feet along and you start debating whether anyone could jump across? Well, it was the boat version of that. The vessel we were on was huge – more like a ferry than something that skips between islands – and our teammate Manu Tuilagi reckoned he could jump off it. There were some Argentinian women on board and my reading was he was trying to impress them. He stripped off to the waist, tattoos on show, as if he was going to jump, but I still wasn't convinced.

'You'll never do it,' I wound him up.

'Why?'

'Well first you can hardly swim and second you just haven't got the bollocks.'

I pulled my hat down over my face and thought that was that. Next thing I heard was a cheer. Then quiet. Then a splash. I pulled my hat up. Louis Deacon was next to me. We looked at each other: 'Fucking hell – he's done it!'

Not only had he done it, but he'd chosen to jump at the exact moment the boat began to turn by the quayside. He was now right by the stern where the propellors were churning through the water. A large crowd had gathered on the shore to see what was going on and I could see police among them. Thank goodness, Manu managed to swim to a nearby pier, but when he emerged he found several none-too-impressed cops waiting to whisk him away to the police station. I ran up there after them, more and more conscious of the fact I was meant to be meeting Steph in an hour's time, and burst in to find an exhausted-looking policewoman on reception.

'I'm here for Manu,' I told her.

'It's going to be a while,' she said.

There were two flights booked for the team, one that night, one the next morning. I lied and told her he was booked on the first. He had to be away that night.

'How long have you been working?' I asked her.

'Fourteen hours,' she replied.

I ran out of the station and found a little coffee house. I returned a few minutes later laden with coffee and cake. It did the trick and Manu was given a pre-charge warning for disorderly behaviour. With my teammate released from behind bars, I legged it back to the hotel. Steph was waiting, but while edging my way towards her I kept being asked for autographs.

'What's going on?' she asked when I finally reached her.

'Oh, apparently I look like one of the England rugby players.'

We sat there and loads of people were still coming over asking me to sign stuff. Steph was watching all the time. Eventually, this bloke said to her, 'You know who he is, don't you?'

'Yeah – Steve Thompson.'

He nodded. 'Steve Thompson who plays for England.'

Finally, the penny dropped. She looked at me – 'You knobhead.'

By March the following year we were married.

That might sound like the definition of a whirlwind romance, and I'm sure we'd have sped headlong into marriage whatever, but by then I had absolutely zero sporting commitments to stand in my way. My life in rugby was dead – gone. I'd left Brive for Leeds Carnegie in 2010. I liked the look of what was happening there under Neil Back, who was much better at coaching than he was at outrunning dogs, but in the end my brief time there didn't turn out as I'd hoped. Leeds, in need of a major overhaul, struggled all season and so I signed a three-year deal with Wasps. Those three years turned out in fact to be sixty minutes. Barely had I put pen to paper than I suffered another devastating neck injury.

Hitting a scrum machine is bread-and-butter training for a front row. On this particular occasion, however, the prop pulled out at the last minute, pulling me sideways. I felt my neck pop as soon as I hit the panel, followed by numbness and nausea. As ever, I tried to convince myself everything was fine and a few days later did actually make my Wasps debut in a win at Worcester. But the area around my neck and shoulder felt horribly uncomfortable. I saw a specialist and he was adamant there was no way back. It wouldn't be safe to carry on playing. It was a massive blow. I was enjoying my rugby and looking forward to writing another chapter in my career at a big club like Wasps, potentially carrying on with England while transitioning to a new life in London that would hopefully throw up plenty of opportunities for when I retired. To have all that turned upside down after a week was gut-wrenching. In a single moment I'd gone from having the next three years of my life mapped out to a void of emptiness.

In need of surgery, I found myself back at the same Bristol hospital under the same doctor who had carried out my first neck operation four years previously. I hoped the engagement wasn't going to be on a permanent cycle like the Olympics. I'm no fan of hospitals and, after he'd done the business in theatre, really didn't want to stay overnight. 'No problem,' said the doc, but as I was waiting to be discharged I suddenly started to feel sweat pouring down my back. Steph had a quick look. All the colour drained from her face. The stitches had popped out and blood was oozing out of the repair.

The doctor had already left for the day but came rushing back. He offered to staple-gun it.

'OK,' I said. 'Do it.' He headed off to find the anaesthetic. 'No, now – just do it!' I was desperate to get out of there. And so that's what he did. Steph's face as the gun crunched was an absolute picture – sickness and horror combined.

With this latest kick in the teeth, what was definitely beyond repair was my love of the game. I'd had it up to there with rugby. Where once it had been a game that picked me up, now it always seemed to leave me mentally and physically on the floor. If I never saw a rugby ball again it would be too soon. I just wanted to get out of that hospital, get on a plane, say bye-bye to rugby and start a new life elsewhere. One door closes and another one opens – that's what they say, isn't it? And I was so lucky that, with Steph, that was exactly what happened. Trouble was, that door led me to two very different destinations. One was a fantastic new future. The other was mental disintegration.

◈

With Steph working for Emirates and my rugby life in England over, it seemed only natural that we should set up our life together in Dubai. I was open to living abroad. I'd spent big chunks of my life overseas and had always invited new experiences, some of which went better than others. A year earlier, for instance, I'd ridden Route 66 from Chicago to Santa Monica on a Triumph Rocket 3. I wanted to look the part and had been nurturing a handlebar moustache and pointy beard while on tour with England in Australia. Added to that I bought a leather waist jacket, denim shorts and 'pisspot' helmet. The finishing touch was a Stars and Stripes bandana. All was going well until, low on fuel, the bike started spluttering. Slowing down, next thing I knew this huge motorcycle convoy was upon me, each rider giving me a very unwelcoming stare as they swept past. At the next petrol station, I pulled in only to see the gang's bikes lined up outside the adjoining café. I filled up but was desperate for a drink, so ventured inside, sticking myself well out of the way in a corner. It didn't work. One of the bikers, massive, covered in tattoos, came over. I was sure I was going to get pulverised, a feeling not helped by the fact I'd recently been watching *Sons of Anarchy*, the blood-splattered outlaw biker gang drama on Netflix. I'll be honest – I was absolutely shitting myself. There was only one thing for it – go English.

'Oh!' I said, looking up at this leather-clad mammoth, 'Terribly sorry. Have I offended you?'

He stared me right in the eyes. 'What are you doing, man?' he asked. 'Why are you here?'

By now *Sons of Anarchy* was beginning to blend with *Deliverance*.

'I'm doing Route 66,' I replied, in my best Queen's English, 'as one does.' I stuck my little finger out while taking a sip from my coffee. 'It's always been a dream of mine, don't you know.'

'Heh!' he turned round to his mates. 'This guy's from Great Britain.'

Well, that was it. Suddenly I was the best friend they'd ever had. 'Heh, do you know a guy called Bob?' (Americans always do this – there's sixty million people in Britain but they seem to think we're all best pals.)

'Bob?'

'Yeah – how's he doing? Haven't seen him for a while.'

'Oh, Bob's fine. He's doing very well.'

'Where you going next?'

'Albuquerque and then on to Flagstaff.'

'Give us your map.' I handed it over and before saying goodbye they ringed a number of restaurants on the route. 'Make sure you go to these,' they advised.

Each one I walked in was the same – 'It's the English guy!' They wouldn't let me pay. The gang had obviously rung ahead and said to make sure I was looked after. If ever those boys are riding the A556 through Cheshire, I'll make sure to do the same.

For me, Dubai offered a new start and I felt I could succeed in a rapidly expanding city offering a multitude of career options. That's exactly what happened as I forged a business development role with a big firm that fitted out high-rise buildings, hotels, department blocks and offices. At the same time, I began helping out other businesses with their manpower needs. I was constantly networking – lunches, dinners, golf – trying to win contracts. I even started a sportswear company, going into schools trying to drum up business. It was how people operated over there. They had a main job and then a dozen other things on the side. For someone who'd never stood still it was perfect. I was out and about doing deals, getting stuff done.

On one occasion I was invited to an event at which I was introduced to Chris Eubank. I think it's safe to say the pleasure was all his. I've been a team member on *A Question of Sport* twice. The first time, Eubank was also a guest and ruined the whole thing by being obstructive and arrogant. As ever he just had to be the centre of attention and sucked all the fun out of the show by creating a really awkward atmosphere.

'You ruined my *Question of Sport*,' I told him. 'You're a knob. Piss off.' I walked away from the bar. Steph was left floundering. She didn't know where to put herself. Funny, I can remember Eubank spoiling that episode clearly – but I have no idea whose team I was on, whether it was with Phil Tufnell or my fellow World Cup winner Matt Dawson.

In Dubai, I'd succeeded in totally reinventing myself, although some things never change. My old coach Matt Bridge, who had a base out there, recalls I used to call in on him at his office, put my feet up on his desk, pick my toenails, and then (old habits die hard) produce an air rifle to shoot the pigeons across the road on the roof. Since, like many sportspeople, I had zero qualifications, and you can count the transferable skills from rugby to real life on one hand, I felt I'd done pretty well. Enthusiasm and energy combined with a whole new life with Steph had delivered a total transformation. Right in front of me I had everything I'd ever wanted – family and security. And then I just stopped.

From nowhere it felt like the positivity and energy had turned into negativity and lethargy. Whereas before I was out networking and socialising five nights a week, and really enjoying it, now I would avoid people, sit alone in restaurants or cafés. I'd feel totally fed up and not want to speak to anyone. The mornings would start off OK, but as the day went on I'd get worse and worse as I got more tired, until I despaired of having to meet anyone. That's where the walls of my life started collapsing. Almost overnight I became paranoid beyond belief. Where once I saw friends, people I'd worked closely with, and formed great professional and personal relationships, I now saw enemies. *They're trying to force me out. Trying to do me over. Trying to get rid of me.* I'd gone from feeling happier and more settled than ever before to a place where I was utterly convinced people were out to get me. That was all that mattered. My mind would be filled with all these dark thoughts. They sat on me day and night like a massive immovable stone. And because I believed I was being pushed away, I made it happen. My attitude – surly, unpredictable, confrontational – meant people didn't want to be around me. My contact book became worthless and my life in Dubai fell apart. My demise was totally self-perpetuating. I built the bomb, lit it, and then stood in front of it when it exploded. But, of course, none of it was my fault.

There was something else that started to happen in Dubai. And it scared me. I'd go into meetings, come out, sit down, and have no memory of anything – what the meeting was about, who was there, what was decided, what I needed to do – anything. I would try all I could to avoid these meetings, but if I really had to attend I'd make an excuse as to why I needed someone else to accompany me. That way I could rely on their memory even if I couldn't rely on my own. I'd justify this amnesia to myself on the basis that it was normal – everybody forgets stuff. But underneath I knew there was more to it. Not only was I forgetting what people said to me, but I was repeating myself to them. More and more often, someone would say, 'You've already told me this.' In the end, I developed a mechanism to deal with it, peppering my speech with, 'I know I've told you this, but . . .'

Steph could only watch and wonder at my character shift. There was no real solid ground on which to base it. I seemed to have everything I wanted. We'd got married, lived in a lovely house, quickly had three beautiful and healthy children in Seren, Slone and Saskia, and I'd made a new career for myself. And yet the Dubai dream had clearly, one way or another, turned sour. In the end, I hit the wall. I'd had enough and just blew. 'I can't stay here. We're leaving.' We quite literally got a map out. Cyprus was the first place we saw. Neither of us had ever been to the island before, but in that moment we decided, 'Right, let's go there – see what happens.' We both enjoyed the sun and Cyprus appeared a good place to relax and sort ourselves out. We rented a house without even seeing it, and within four weeks had moved to Peyia, a seaside town on the west coast.

In my head it felt so right. I wanted to be around my family. I'd been working such long hours in Dubai that I'd barely seen Steph and the kids. But before long, the blue skies again started to turn grey. Instead of throwing myself into this second chance, I did nothing but sit in the garden. I barely socialised and hardly did anything with the kids. Steph has said it a few times – 'I just didn't know what to do with you.' I was aware enough to know my behaviour wasn't what it should be, but other than that had no idea what was going on. I didn't think it was depression or low mood or anything like that, I just thought I had become a miserable prick. That's the thing. You can have everything, a great life, all that goes with it, but sunshine, a nice house, lovely surroundings, a fantastic family is no protection from what's going on in your head.

It's weird, but one of the few things that did make me happy in Cyprus was the cars. Everywhere I looked were all the old vehicles of my youth. I found it strangely comforting. Knowing what I know now, I can't help thinking how people with dementia find similar comfort in nostalgia, to the extent that some care homes decorate doors and walls with familiar images from years ago.

By now, money was getting tight. People think top-level sport provides an automatic safety net; that it sets you up for life. But it doesn't always work like that. There was a moment in Cyprus where I checked our finances and realised all we had in the world was £3.86. That's not a safety net. It's a tightrope over shark-infested waters. I picked up bits of work here and there to keep us ticking over, but life had gone from easy and carefree to trudge and struggle.

To this day it upsets me massively that, while I was out

there, Keith Picton died. Keith had been such an incredible figure in my life, someone I loved and respected dearly, and I couldn't even afford to get back to England for his funeral. They say that the transition back into civvy street is a leveller for a lot of sportspeople. For me, that moment of desperate realisation illustrated the truth more than any other. It sent me even further into a downward spiral. I thought of Keith giving me the money for fish and chips when I was skint on the team bus that time. Now, twenty years on, I couldn't even rustle up the money to say a proper goodbye. I would give anything to change that situation. I feel ashamed and it eats me up inside. I hope, Keith, you can forgive me.

In the end, it was clear that Cyprus was never going to be the answer to the question of where to make our long-term future. Money worries aside, I had enough self-awareness to know that mentally I was in a bad place. Cyprus wasn't working and neither was I. By comparison, the UK offered a comfort blanket, a chance to start again in familiar surroundings. Heading home didn't need to feel like the end of an adventure when it so clearly offered the chance of a new beginning for us and our now four children – Saxon had joined the gang in Cyprus.

◈

Looking back over this period, while I'm not looking for excuses for behaviour that caused family upheaval and the loss of valued friendships and working relationships, I am once again drawn to the knowledge I have now – that head injuries spark decisions that would in so many other ways make absolutely no sense. People I knew in Dubai repeatedly talk about me changing from one person to another. I've read it about others in the same brain damage boat: 'They just turned into a totally different person.' Certainly, that would explain a few situations I've been in, and why, while before if someone messed me about, that was it, done, I've recently started to wonder if I might need to say sorry to a few people. At the same time, those I trust implicitly tell me that by going straight from sport into the particularly harsh business environment of Dubai, I was essentially entering a 'snake pit' blindfold. There were plenty of people out there ready and willing to bite, to take advantage of someone with a lack of business nous.

The lack of real understanding as to how and why those relationships slipped beneath the water is something I have to live with. Those demons will always sit on my shoulder, jostling for position with all the others. Only certainty can ever make them go away. Unfortunately, if I don't have certainty now then it's hardly likely to drop down in the next shower.

Not knowing about the future is one thing. Not knowing about the past means you can never quite put it to bed. All I can do is be in the present and hope to be aware.

Chapter 11

HAVE I GOT IT?

It was Alix Popham, the former Wales back-row forward, and an old teammate of mine at Brive, who first got me really wondering about the state of my brain. Alix had started out in the pro game around the same time as me. A no-nonsense player, known for his tough tackling and one hundred per cent commitment, he was the sort of bloke every coach would want on their team. In retirement, Alix, like me, is a devoted family man. I'd always known him as a really laid-back kind of guy. But, as we chatted on the phone one day, he began talking quite deeply. He told me he couldn't remember his career. He described how his personality had changed, how he would forget names, words, the simplest of things. He found it hard to concentrate and was prone to inexplicable mood swings and episodes of anxiety. There were times out of nowhere he felt aggressive and angry. I couldn't believe what I was hearing. It was as if he was talking about me.

Eventually, after getting lost on a bike ride he'd done dozens of times before, with no idea where he was or how to get home, Alix had sought medical help. He'd undergone scans and the end result was to be diagnosed with early-onset dementia due to damage sustained to his brain. Forever in the thick of it, Alix reckons he took more than 100,000 hits in his career. No wonder he's struggling.

'You were a physical player,' he said. 'You should go and get yourself checked out as well.' As he was telling me about his symptoms, my plan straight away was to do exactly that. If ticking boxes marked memory loss, confusion, irritability, anger, depression and an inability to concentrate meant a likelihood of suffering from early-onset dementia, I was definitely in the mix. But then as soon as he rang off, my mindset switched back to *There's nothing to worry about. I'm all right. Everything's fine.*

Alix, though, got a specialist to phone me up. For ninety minutes I sat in the works van while he asked me different questions about my experiences and tested my responses to set questions that would reveal tell-tale signs as to how my brain was functioning. He called me back later after checking his notes. 'There might be a problem,' he said.

I was introduced to Richard Boardman, a solicitor building a case for negligence against the rugby authorities, and scans were organised that would definitely show the state of my brain. There was no pressure at all to join the case. That was left entirely up to me. Richard had got in touch because Alix had told him about me. I can genuinely say all anyone wanted to do at that stage was check I was all right. When I learned more about what Richard was trying to do and the basis on which the case was built – that those in the rugby HQs had failed to act on clear evidence of the risks of head injury – I made the decision to jump on board.

A specialist came out to the house to do some cognitive tests. She gave me puzzles where I had to fit different shapes together. Then she'd show me a picture, turn it over and ask me to draw what I'd seen. I would think I'd done OK but then she'd turn the original image back over and I'd be nowhere near. I kept apologising – 'I'm so sorry' – part out of embarrassment and part out of disbelief at how bad I was doing. A word test followed. She'd say twenty words and I had to try to remember them and repeat them. It was the most awful feeling. She'd say the first two words, and I'd remember them, and then she'd say the third and the first two would disappear. We'd do other puzzles while occasionally returning to the word game. It was the same twenty words every time, but the most I could ever remember was five. The competitive side of me kicked in. *Pull yourself together. Stay calm. Do this properly. Get the best score you can.* But you can't compete against brain damage.

It upset me massively. I knew my memory was going. I'd seen it at work. I'd go back to the van for some tools and by the time I pulled open the door I would have no idea what I was meant to be fetching. But to have the problem highlighted like this, stuff just not going in at all, was horrible. It really brought it home to me how bad I was. I felt panicky – *this is the truth of what's happening to me* – to the extent the specialist actually had to calm me down. There were proper tears, proper crying, and I actually had to go upstairs to take time out and reset myself.

Later, I travelled down to King's College London for a diffusion tensor imaging (DTI) scan, which detects progressive brain injury in a way not visible on a conventional magnetic resonance imaging (MRI) scan that more generally maps the condition of the brain. I've always been confident travelling round London but this time the Underground made me feel like a rat in a maze. I sat there and started to panic. I kept thinking I was going the wrong way or, worse, was so gripped by confusion that I had no idea where I was. I could see people looking at me. *Is this weirdo psyching out?* I used to enjoy the Tube for the people-watching. Now it felt like every set of eyes was on me. A couple of times I jumped off at stations so I could look at the map on the wall and reassure myself I was going the right way. I felt like I was in a different world to anything I'd ever previously experienced when in fact I'd done this without even thinking about it so many times. Nowadays, if I go down to London I walk everywhere. I get to Euston early, make sure I'm never rushed, and take a gentle stroll. Even if my destination is an hour away, I'll still walk. I won't put myself under needless stress or pressure.

Like most sportspeople I'd been in MRI scanners before, but the DTI was different. I still had to be slid into the machine, but now my head was screwed down in a clamp. Not that it bothered me for long. I'm a bit of a medical oddball in that as soon as I'm shoved in a scanner, the whirring puts me to sleep. I've always seen a scan as the deepest sleep you could ever have. I told the staff, but they didn't believe me – until within seconds my snores confirmed I was dead to the world. This wasn't ideal as the scan lasted an hour and parts of it needed to capture me in a waking state. Every now and then, I'd be woken up by a voice: 'Steve! Steve! Wake up! You need to be awake for these next few minutes.'

'OK, no problem!' The next noise they heard was me snoring again.

'Steve!' I'm the same on a plane or if I'm a passenger in a car – gone within the minute.

Not helped by Covid, the results seemed to take weeks. All the time, my mind was flipping from a panicked – *They're going to find something* – to a more balanced– *It's going to be fine.* I went through periods where I was convinced I was OK – *There's nothing wrong with my brain – I'm just stupid!* And then I'd think, *But if there's nothing wrong with me, how come I did so badly on that test?* Other times I'd put it down to age. I mean, we all start forgetting stuff, don't we? But then that couldn't be right either. I was forty-two. If I was seventy-two or eighty-two maybe that would be the case. Eventually, I had a message from Richard Boardman.

'We've got your results.'

'OK,' I replied. 'What do they say?'

He didn't feel he was the one who should tell me. 'The specialist will call you tomorrow.'

'What? Tomorrow?' I didn't want to wait until tomorrow. Why would anyone want to wait until tomorrow to find out if they've got dementia? It's not like hanging on for an Amazon delivery. I couldn't go the whole night without knowing. How the hell were Steph and I supposed to sleep?

I was insistent. 'Just message me now in simple terms. Have I got dementia or not?'

A few seconds later I heard a ping. I looked at my phone. There was one word on the screen. 'Yes.'

I've told a few people this and more often than not they're amazed I should have been told in such a blunt way. But then they remember, *Oh, hang on, it's Steve. That's exactly what he'll have wanted.* I'm not the type who needs to be sat down in a chair with a cup of tea and a hanky.

'Apologies,' Richard came back, 'the doctor will articulate what that means.'

Next day came the call from the specialist. 'You might want to sit down,' he told me.

Despite myself, I pulled up a chair. 'OK, I'm sitting down.'

'You've got a lot of damage to your brain.'

I'd been diagnosed with early-onset dementia, plus suspected CTE – suspected because it could only be confirmed by a knife being taken to my lifeless brain. This isn't the sort of news generally delivered to a patient by phone, but Covid got in the way. That meant the expert couldn't talk me through the scan person to person. Instead, the inside of my head arrived via email attachment. The healthy parts of my brain would be grey, I was told, the dead bits would be yellow. I opened the attachment. There was a lot of yellow. I wasn't expecting that but, while it was undeniably shocking, neither Steph nor I really knew what it meant.

'Has anyone ever had anything like this from a one-off incident?' Steph asked, hoping against hope it might not be linked to an endless succession of brain injuries over time; that it might not actually be too bad, potentially recoverable.

'Oh yes,' replied the expert. 'I've seen this in a one-off incident.'

'Oh right,' she said, a little relieved, 'that's good.'

'No, no,' he said, 'it was a car accident. The person was dead. Someone with that much damage from a one-off event is gone.'

CTE, it was explained, is caused by repeated blows to the head. The repetitive nature of the injury meant my body had adapted to survive. If I'd sustained that much damage in one go, I wouldn't have been having the conversation. The good news – that I wasn't dead – ended pretty much there. My damage might have been progressive, but dementia, mood swings and memory loss would be the result.

When the call ended, I don't think either of us could believe that what we'd just heard was real. In fact, we just carried on as normal, stuck the kettle on and had a cup of tea. I know it sounds ridiculous, but, if anything, I was massively relieved – *I haven't gone stupid, there is something there.* I was quite literally high on adrenaline – *Yes, I get it! I've got this!*

It was the sheer relief of knowing what was wrong with me. My behaviour wasn't me being odd, or an arsehole – this was an actual condition with symptoms and a name. Also, while the specialist had used the words 'early-onset dementia and probable CTE', mentally I had skimmed over the dementia element. Because it was termed 'early onset' I saw it as just meaning I'd only got it a tiny bit, or I might get it properly in the future.

I think partly my crazily euphoric reaction was delayed shock. This strange high that came with clear knowledge soon disappeared. A couple of hours later we were both thinking the same thing – *Oh shit.* I read up on early-onset dementia and found what it really meant was I'd got it young, way before it could ever reasonably be expected to afflict my mind. We started asking ourselves, 'How do we fix this?' We couldn't find an answer. You can't fix brain cells that are dead.

Within days I had sunk into a deep, deep low as the true ramifications of the diagnosis came crashing down. *What have I got the kids into? What have I got Steph into? She met me when I'd just finished playing and now she's paying the price for all the years she wasn't even part of. And it can only get worse.*

Thing is, while knowing what's wrong with you is empowering in that it gives you something to rally against, it's no barrier against the actual illness. Dementia just keeps coming. There have been a couple of times where I've been driving and literally just come to a standstill. I look around me and have no idea where I am or where I'm going. It's hard at a time like that not to panic – *What's going on? Where am I?* I challenge anyone unlucky enough to find themselves in that situation not to do the same. I mean, how can you literally lose all awareness of your surroundings? To be totally lost like that is terrifying. It's like every reference point you've ever had has been stripped away. You see everyone else carrying on with their business while you are in an absolute internal panic. Such a lonely place to be. You might as well have been cast adrift in the middle of the sea. There's an online game where you're randomly placed anywhere in the world on Google Maps and have to work out where you are. That's OK in a game. In the real world it's a nightmare, and like a nightmare your only hope of escape is that your brain will click into action and wake you up.

I understand I have to know what's wrong with me if I'm to give myself the best chance, but equally there's a huge part of me that wishes I'd never known. That I'd never heard of CTE, of court cases, of my mind ebbing away. That way I could be getting on with my life blissfully unaware of the situation, just thinking I was getting a bit forgetful, that I get moody every now and again because of stress. *I could have lived happily oblivious*, I think to myself. *I could have saved all this upset for when I got really bad.*

Who would I have been kidding?

Chapter 12

MOODY BASTARD

I like to go fishing on the Manchester Ship Canal. It's headspace, a chance either to escape from what's happening to me or to sit quietly and, as best as I can, think it through.

Except today as I walk along to my usual spot, this cold April morning, rain in the air, cloak of grey cloud, I'm suddenly overwhelmed by how tired I feel.

'I've had enough,' I think. 'I'm exhausted. There's not much more I can take.'

The water looks beckoning.

'Jump in there,' I say to myself, 'and it will all be over. It will swallow me up and slowly I'll drift away.'

◈

I had a nickname at Northampton Saints – Bipolar Wal. I was never diagnosed as bipolar, maybe because I never went to see anyone about my ups and downs, and people just said it as a piss-take. But maybe they were closer to the mark than any of us ever knew. How else do you explain someone who one minute is bouncing off the ceiling and the next is in the depths of despair, a proper moody bastard? Now those mood swings are more magnified than ever. One minute, I'm happy, positive, loving life, the next I'm sat on the edge of the bed with my head in my hands. Sounds mad, I know, but in those moments I can fathom no actual reason behind that complete U-turn in character. In fact, when I'm on my knees the worst thing anyone can say to me is, 'Why are you in a mood?' That in itself irritates me. I don't need a trigger. I don't need something to have happened at work or to have had a falling-out. I just am. *So why ask?*

I've come to see myself as living on a spiral staircase. At the top is a place where I can feel happiness, where I can revel in the family life I'm so lucky to have been given. Down at the bottom is where my darkest thoughts reside. *I could end this right now, and then the kids won't have to live with a dad who's like Jekyll and Hyde.* It would help if thoughts like that were a bit out there – removed from the reality of life. But, sadly, they make sense. No child should wake up and think, *I wonder what mood Dad's going to be in today.*

I don't want that to be their life but I can't keep my mental state stable. I have no defence from a downer sweeping in. All I can do if one gathers on the horizon is try to put a bit of distance between myself and the kids. I don't want them to see me in a hole, so I'll go for a workout, or grab my rod and head out fishing, something I absolutely must have in my life. I love the release it gives me, or at least I do most of the time.

Given time to dwell, I sometimes start to overthink my situation and really start questioning *What's the point?* So much of my life has been a fight. I worry that the next kick in the teeth will be the last I can take. I've always been single-minded and done whatever it takes, so I know it's in me to make a decision. One step and it could all be gone. That's not great when you're stood in front of the wide expanse of water that is the Manchester Ship Canal. Equally, however, that time away will soon have me missing Steph and the kids. Walk through the door to the sight of Saxon pulling one of his weird faces and I'm immediately sucked out of my low mood.

When you're younger, life is full of highs and lows. It's inevitable. You're doing more. You're experiencing things for the first time. You find yourself in unpredictable situations. Some will work out, some will be a failure. Get older, though, and you want a smoother ride. And that's how I want my life now with Steph and the kids. There are going to be some serious bumps further along the road, so all of us need to enjoy a stable life while we can. Standing in the way of that is exhaustion – from the ups just as much as the downs. In those better moments I feel I can take on the world. I feel amazing. I want to be part of everything. And then suddenly – crash – I'm down on the canvas again. I now also have something else to contend with. In those good moments, buzzing with energy, I'll have organised stuff –

days out, meeting friends, trips to events – 'Let's do it. It'll be amazing!' – and then by the time the actual day comes around I'll be right back down again.

Even the simplest things can spark a level of anxiety in me that just should never be there. Before Covid hit, for example, we thought about going to a Christmas fayre – lights, food, music, everyone having a great time together. No one used to love getting out doing things more than me, and when we first talked about the fayre I couldn't wait. It sounded amazing and I knew the kids would love it. But the closer the event came, the more I was consumed by fear. And I mean fear. The mere thought of it sent my nervousness through the roof. I'd have rather cut off a hand than go anywhere near it. Steph knew by then that if she confronted me I'd become even more belligerent and retreat into myself. I'd start looking for excuses to have an argument; make it so she was the reason I wouldn't go – 'Fine. I'm not interested any more, go by yourself' – when really it was me being an arsehole. OK, actually my reluctance to do things is a symptom of the dementia, but it feels like I'm being an arsehole to me. Not that I ever want to use the dementia as an all-encompassing excuse for my behaviour. I'm perfectly capable of being an arsehole without it being the result of illness. Dementia isn't a trump card to play when things get difficult.

My fear means Steph and the kids often end up going to things without me. I'll stay at home on my own. I find no respite from the mental anguish though. The second that front door shuts I'm overwhelmed with guilt. Shame is my only companion. *What sort of husband and dad am I that I've just done that to them?* I'll look at a photo of us all on the wall and think to myself, *How have you ended up with me?* Just the same as I'm sure there have been times when Steph has lain awake in bed at 3am and wondered *What have you got yourself into with him?* She and the kids are constantly having to adapt around me. In any normal house no way should that be the case. A dad adapts around his family, not the other way round.

Problem is I find the prospect of being around people unnerving. I don't like queues, being in busy bars, stuff like that. Immediately, I'll get a headache. *Why am I here? I just want to get out. I just want to get away.* If I have to be somewhere busy, I'll find the furthest, quietest corner. I'll sit there and wonder, *Why did I put myself in this position?* And I know it'll probably be because I organised it or agreed to it when I was on a mental high.

To anyone who knows me, it's one of the most obvious changes in my behaviour. I used to be really sociable, whereas now, as something starts getting nearer in the diary I start searching for ways and reasons to avoid it, hoping someone will ring and say it's been cancelled. *Please text. Please say you can't make it. That you've double-booked. That there's something wrong with your car.* That feeling of dread can come over me at any time. I went on a bike ride with Hephs recently. I was bang up for it when it was organised but as it got nearer and nearer, I was absolutely shitting myself. The thought of traffic, lorries, coming past me freaked me out. *What's happened to you?* I asked myself. *You used to be fearless. You were full throttle.*

You wouldn't give a shit about anything, and now suddenly you're
scared of going out on a pushbike on a road?

As bad as it sounds, I was like a pig in shit during Covid
because I didn't have to do anything. I had a ready-made
excuse that covered everything. Once lockdown finished,
I had a night out arranged in London and was absolutely
dreading it. I had to really make myself go, and actually had
a fantastic time. But that's the thing with feeling low, your
brain tricks you into thinking that the things that are good
for you are in fact your enemy. Thankfully, myself and Steph
have both come to recognise that scenario unfolding. She'll
give me a bit of room to calm down and help me get myself
together so I feel more at ease with going somewhere. It's that
initial step, like going over the edge when you're abseiling.
She knows that once I'm there, so long as it's an environment
I find comfortable, I'll more often than not have a really good
time. Steph and I went to a wedding recently and had the
best weekend ever. The other day we went out for a curry
and were loving it so much we were at the table for three and
a half hours, playing I-spy and being silly with the kids. We
were all there together and I just wanted it to last forever. I
know people say life's not like that, but for us it's so important
that it is. Forever for us might not be very long.

◈

Everyone changes with age, I get that. But I'm not sure that
age, at least getting into your forties, destroys confidence
and generates anxiety at the levels that I experience. In the

past I'd go shopping a bit like I'd won *Supermarket Sweep*, not quite one arm out shovelling everything into my trolley but certainly pretty carefree. Now I'll go down there and spend ten minutes seeing which loaf has got the latest sell-by date. That can be seen as sensible, but it's more than that – I can't walk away until I know. I used to take the piss out of people obsessed with things like that and now I'm one of them. Except while perhaps some people are doing it out of necessity, saving every penny they can, I'm doing it because I've gone into a state of panic. I'm worrying about something that doesn't bother me, and am totally aware it doesn't matter, but there's nothing I can do to stop myself. It's got to the stage now where I rarely do any shopping. I'm nervous about how I won't be able to stop myself acting in a certain manner. That's without the discomfort of having all those other shoppers around me. To me, these days, a few people in an aisle at Tesco feels like 82,000 packed into Twickenham.

I'm sure I must seem a shadow of my former self. Lewis used to describe me as always being the last to go home on a night out, radar forever honed to find the last bar open. I remember after England played Italy in Rome in 2010 going over to the Italian team hotel to see my Brive teammate Valerio Bernabò. I couldn't help but admire the array of police motorcycles lined up outside. When I saw the keys had been left in one of them, that was it, I was off. Well, I had a motorbike licence so why not? I was up and down the road on this proper big police motorbike. Absolutely brilliant, and all things considered the Italian police were very good about it.

I know I was that person, but if I think back to those times now it seems unreal, a dream. Or a nightmare if it was a night out with Lewis! I can see myself but I'm not really there. The old 'try anything' Steve has disappeared, replaced by one of apprehension and uncertainty. I used to travel all over the world – go anywhere at the drop of a hat. I'd jump on my motorbike and drive off into the middle of nowhere, shoot off for business meetings across the globe. And now I'm panicking about being on a pushbike if a hatchback gets a little too close. Steph says to me, 'It's as if a light has gone out,' and I know exactly what she means. Instead of taking life as it comes, everything has to be organised. Whatever it is I'm doing, big or small, the unknown isn't an option. I need knowledge, an itinerary. Any niggling doubts and it's not happening – not with me involved anyway. I don't want any unknowns to dwell on, because they can all too easily send me plummeting down. I don't want to feel way low any more than I want to feel sky-high – because I know now that with any big upper usually comes an equally big downer. And knowing that's coming is almost as bad as the downer itself. All I want these days is a flat line somewhere in the middle; something that feels like normal. If having order in my life – my quieter life – makes that happen then that's fine with me. I don't aspire to have any more big moments. My life is Steph and the kids, making sure they're OK. That's why being calm, a 40-watt bulb instead of a glaring spotlight, is so important to me. Ups and downs I can live without. Down equals dangerous. Wrong place, wrong time, and a down can be very bad news indeed.

In some ways, the new version of me has been a benefit. I used to get bad road rage but in the last couple of years it's all changed and now I'm completely the opposite. While I get anxious before a journey, the minute I get in the car it completely vanishes. It's become a relaxing space. Quite literally, I live life in the slow lane. On the motorway I'm quite happy to sit on the inside carriageway with the caravans and lorries listening to all my favourite real-crime podcasts – the way I am means I can listen to them again and again and never know who did it or what's going to happen! I enjoy my motorbike as well, again in a bit less full-on way than I might have before. A motorbike for me now is just about freedom, taking my time. Fire up the engine and I have an instant smile. I've come to recognise what works for me; what puts me in a peaceful frame of mind. I've got things I can reach for in the knowledge they'll give me some respite.

There are other ways to balance mood but I don't like the idea of anti-depressants controlling me and my emotions. 'Happy pills' scare me. I don't want to be knocked out, to miss out on real life, to be zombified. They say it's wrong to see anti-depressants as a bad thing, that for millions they're a positive, but until I understand exactly what it is that's happening to me and my brain, I really don't feel comfortable adding anti-depressants into the mix. I'd rather find some sort of settled state another way.

The fact I'm even talking about my mental health is a milestone I never thought I'd reach. Never, actually, wanted to reach. I'd always been one of those people who totally dismissed talk of mental health issues. *What a load of bollocks. Why don't people just shut up and get on with it.* I was the classic 'Man up!' character. I couldn't comprehend how anyone lucky enough to play sport for a living, or in fact be in a good position in life full-stop, could possibly describe themselves as down or depressed. My view was they were just being soft or seeing an off-day for more than it was.

Let's face it, there's no more alpha sport in the world than rugby. Certainly, in my day there was no chance a player might sit in a changing room and start talking about deep inner feelings. It just wasn't done. I've seen blokes whose marriages have broken down ribbed mercilessly. 'What happened, mate? Some bloke have a bigger dick than you?' The person on the end of that would know their mates were there for them really, but even so that's a hell of a culture to go against. Male sport was just not a touchy-feely environment. Even if you did have the self-awareness to conclude you might have a mental health issue, no way would you shout up. On a simple functional day-to-day basis, show any kind of 'weakness' and you might lose your place in the team. Hide it and slide deeper and deeper into secret distress was the only answer. What's happened to me has taught me that environment is toxic. Anyone, anywhere, is capable of being consumed by depression, and comparing it to just having a 'bad day' is like comparing a stubbed toe to a broken back.

Feeling mentally destroyed is akin to drowning at the bottom of a dark well. You can't imagine ever being able to breathe freely again, let alone see a glimpse of light.

I'll be honest; at times I feel a complete failure. I don't have *Why me?* moments. I have *I must deserve it* moments. I believe in what goes around comes around. *This must be karma. I must have been a complete c*** when I was younger.* Somehow, if I'm to keep going, I have to resist those kinds of thoughts. They're the ones that could drag me under. Thankfully, so far, amidst the wreckage of my mind, the spirit that helped me through my early years has somehow survived to keep me afloat. My overriding instinct, for now at least, is to look dementia in the eye – and fight.

Chapter 13

RESISTANCE

Seren was at a party at a friend's house the other day. When we picked her up, the little girl's mum told us how quiet she'd been – until the Wii came out. That was it, she was off. No way was anyone going to beat her.

'Good girl,' I told her when she got in the car. Later, at dinner, I went to fist-bump her at the table. Steph gave me a stare. 'Don't you dare!'

I'm not proud of that episode (actually, that's not true – I am proud of that episode) but it shows that Seren is a chip off the old block. Like most people who reach the top in sport, I'm highly competitive. And never have I needed that drive more than now. Dementia is the toughest, most unforgiving opponent I will ever have. It is also, ultimately, unbeatable. Top of the league, reigning champion. The winner that stays on, time after time.

I'm fortunate enough never to have known anyone with dementia. It's something you might come across with an older family member, but of course never seeing any of my relatives, elderly or otherwise, that doesn't apply to me. But I do know that dementia is an old person's illness – right? It's something that affects people sat around in care homes staring blankly at game shows on TV while strangers – once loved ones – search for a flicker of recognition. It's someone wandering the street in their nightclothes. It's an incontinent old man not even aware they've wet themselves. I don't want that to happen to me any more than I'm sure they didn't want it to happen to them. Maybe they too knew their fate early in the drama. Maybe they too hoped against hope that the onslaught could be reversed. Perhaps they too asked, 'How do I fight dementia?' It's a question that more and more of us will have to face. I just wasn't expecting to be asking the question quite so early in life.

In rugby, I soon found that to compete you need more than skill – you need a mindset. You also need, at some point, aggression. To say otherwise is nonsensical. Rugby pitches two teams of deeply committed individuals – people who believe themselves to be winners – against one another. Within that set-up is an intense loyalty to teammates driven by the game itself, demanding as it does that players and positions must protect one another if they are to succeed. Teams often find aggression is a shortcut to the total commitment the sport demands, and I would put hatred in the same bracket. Early in my career I played for England

Under-19s at Cardiff. I couldn't believe what I was seeing. There were grown men leaning over the hoardings spitting at us, calling us every name in the book. As someone who'd lived a blinkered life in Northampton and hadn't seen much of life in the wider world, that game was the biggest eye-opener I could have ever had. I really saw the hate they had for us. I don't know what everyone else was thinking, but I had one thought; *Why can't we hate them as much as they hate us?* And from that point on that's exactly what I did. I built myself up to absolutely hate the opposition, and other players did exactly the same. As much as other teams built their own hate against England, we would always out-hate them back. It gave us an added edge. The French were always strong mentally and physically, but with the hate we knew we could overpower them. Whoever the opposition, that successful England team of the early 2000s was especially good at building the loathing.

In the days before a game, if we played Scotland, for example, we'd focus on their big players and just pour bile on them. We had to – because we knew they'd be doing exactly the same to us. Too often the English are hindered by reserve. In some circles, 'hate' is a dirty word. A Scotland player says he hates the English and it's seen as pride, as passion. An English person says the same about the Scots and someone will inevitably turn round and say, 'You can't say that. It's disgusting.' It happened during the Six Nations in 2020. Scotland centre Sam Johnson vented his spleen against the English, but when England's Lewis Ludlam started using the 'H' word, people piled in saying it was inappropriate. You can't allow your opponent to gain that extra 10 per cent while you're left behind. They might enter the field with that hate in their armoury, but as soon as they see you have it too their weapon is null and void. Already you have left a mark on them. They can see exactly how much you want it; to what extent you are willing to go in order to achieve your goal. In recent years I have seen England teams playing with the attitude of 'we deserve to win'. Go into a contest thinking you're owed something and you will lose. You have to want to win – really want to win. While teams such as Scotland and Wales do occasionally have good squads, they shouldn't ever beat England who massively outmatch them for a selection pool of players and resources. But the truth is they do get one over us because they want it more.

The mere act of being a sportsperson doesn't make someone special. Some people are so self-important because they play sport, when actually there will be plenty of others out there just as good or even better – they just never had the breaks. Not everyone has an awareness of that type of thing. Some people have an expectation that things will slot into place; everything will go their way. And they're the ones who, just when they're not expecting it, tend to get the biggest kick up the arse.

My own drive to come out on top sometimes led to a bit of underhand activity. Not getting caught was always part of life in the front row. When he was director of rugby at Saints, John Steele once told me the citing commissioner, an independent official responsible for identifying players who commit acts of foul play, knew I was up to stuff but just couldn't catch me. Getting involved in scraps was just part of the game, and the good thing about rugby was there were legal ways of giving people a dig. A friend pointed out to me recently that in the World Cup semi-final in 2003 I broke one of the French props' ribs with my shoulder in a maul – fine at the time. Again, looks bad on paper, but out there on the pitch, if you didn't do it to them they'd most certainly do it to you.

If I thought it would improve my game, I'd take a source of hate from anywhere. I'd watch the All Blacks perform the Haka and think, *You're going to get it!* The hollering, the posturing – it didn't intimidate me; if anything it built me up. But I didn't need it to get the blood pumping. I could hate someone from nowhere. Insert yourself into this scenario. I'm sitting with you having a nice quiet coffee. You then nip to the toilet and while you're away someone tells me you're in the opposition team at the weekend. From that second on I will absolutely despise you. I will build so much hate in my mind that when the game comes round I will want to steamroller you, crush you into little pieces. Put like that, it sounds awful, but as a professional you take whatever you can to level out that playing field.

Rugby, for me, is long gone. Aside from keeping an eye on how England are getting on, it doesn't really feature in my life. But dementia very definitely does, and that is now my fight, one that again will take a lot of inner strength, especially with the knowledge that ultimately I can never come out on the winning side. Most times, you take a problem to a doctor in the hope they can give you a cure. With CTE there is no cure. It's too late. The brain's decline is on an unstoppable course. All you can really do is accept its presence and, as best you can, while you can, try to hold back the tide.

As soon as I heard the letters CTE, I wanted to learn more. I wanted to check my opponent out. Initially, that led me to the film *Concussion* in which Will Smith stars as Bennet Omalu, a forensic pathologist in the US who, through painstaking work, uncovered the link between CTE and American football. Omalu investigated the brains of ex-players whose behaviour in the years up to their deaths had become increasingly erratic, most notably Pittsburgh Steelers legend and four-times Super Bowl winner Mike Webster. In retirement, the man known to all as 'Iron Mike' appeared to lose all sense of control. He could be wildly unpredictable and aggressive and ended up living rough on the streets of the city that had once worshipped him. Never able to switch off, he was known to Taser himself into unconsciousness to get some sleep. Mike Webster died aged just fifty. Omalu analysed his brain in microscopic detail. It resembled that of a man who had been in multiple car crashes. He was the first NFL player to be diagnosed with CTE.

I don't want to end up like Mike Webster – but I already am. I have looked through my medical records and there are a lot of big head injuries in there. That's without all the lesser ones, the sub-concussions, heaped on top. More concerning was Webster's behaviour. He might have been at the more extreme end of the repercussions of CTE, but even so there were enough familiarities – mood changes in particular – for me to wonder, and fear, how my character might regress over the coming years. The children already say that when I shout they want to get out of the way. I hate the thought that I might scare them, but I know as well that sometimes I just can't help but react in a certain manner. Often I feel utterly lost as to why I'm behaving in such a stupid way. I really don't know any more than anyone else. What might to anyone else seem a mild frustration – a spilt drink or a snapped lace – will make me blow up like a volcano. I physically can't help myself, the same as your lower leg involuntarily jerks if a doctor taps you at a certain point on the knee. Things like that frighten me. I don't want to be like that now, so I certainly don't want to get any worse.

It's a part of dementia that a lot of people either don't know about or don't consider, but you don't have to look far to find stories of the calmest of individuals flipping over into behaviour that is totally out of character. Sadly, CTE has put a lot of people, sporting and otherwise, in a dark place. I have seen and read about how it has sparked some players in the NFL to be violent to those around them. I've spoken to rugby players – people who are the most laid-back characters you could meet – who've punched holes in walls. That scares me massively. Surely I won't ever be the same?

The most infamous sporting CTE sufferer, the former New England Patriots tight end Aaron Hernandez, killed himself while serving a life sentence for murder. Naturally, the discovery of CTE in Hernandez's brain led to speculation over how his behaviour might have been adversely affected by the condition. Not everybody with CTE murders people, but if it's enough to make even one person act in such a sickeningly violent way, then it's only natural that, if it's strongly suspected you have the same illness, you will feel a bit unsettled. Millions will finish the Netflix documentary *Killer Inside: The Mind of Aaron Hernandez*, make a cup of tea, sit back down and calmly look around for their next box-set binge. When I watch programmes like that, I can't rest. I feel a knot inside.

The list of NFL players to have taken their own lives after repeated brain injuries is long. Two players, Dave Duerson and Junior Seau, actually shot themselves in the chest so their brains could be put to use by those researching CTE. Doubters tried to claim that Duerson shot himself because he was afflicted by depression. They couldn't see that it was the head trauma he'd suffered that had caused that decline in his mental health in the first place. I read about sportspeople committing suicide and it makes me feel normal, because, like on the canal bank and the train platform, I have had those thoughts as well. Think about that – I have reached a stage where dead people make me feel less alone.

Behavioural changes will happen, just the same as my cognitive abilities will decline. Naturally, I want to put off both for as long as possible. There's no individual road map for dementia that doesn't ultimately peter out into the unknown, so I can't say how I'm going to change as a person any more than I can say I'll need care in five, ten or fifteen years' time. For the moment, though, I can think clearly enough to give myself as big a chance as possible to fend off the day when I'm left with zero control of my character.

Physically, bizarrely, I'm just about as good as I've ever been. Yes, I'm carrying around past knocks, but I'm not constantly getting injured and patched up as part of daily life. I ride hundreds of miles on my Peloton exercise bike, have an outdoors job, and am in the fresh air all the time playing with the kids and walking the dog. It's not just the physical benefits, exercise helps me mentally, too. When I start feeling anxious and stressed, I can get on the Peloton and know it will give me an escape. I don't pile into exercise. I don't drag up memories of the dreaded Bernard at Brive and half kill myself to find that release. I see ex-sportspeople who take that body-crunching mentality into retirement, absolutely hammering themselves in the gym, and have no wish to step back into that kind of murderous regime. I prefer my approach – push yourself, but appreciate and enjoy what you're doing at the same time. That way, instead of feeling like a wreck, you come away mentally refreshed.

There's another reason I rarely push myself hard – it can click something in my head. It makes my skull feel like it's full of cotton wool. I can't risk tipping my brain over into an uncomfortable state. I have to keep it clear if it's to operate to a good level. From that point of view, I was lucky that, after reading about my problems, former London Welsh and

Rosslyn Park rugby player James Strong got in touch. James, who's had his own fair share of knocks, is a pioneer in red light therapy. The wavelength of red light penetrates deeper into the body than that of other colours and has been shown to decrease recovery times from injuries, reduce inflammation and encourage the body's repair system. Brain inflammation is a central feature of dementia and so every day I sit between two screens of red lights. They're like a screenwash for the mind, and with that clarity comes an ability to think and see more positively. Just sitting in the dark with the lights next to me is soothing. Another hangover from brain trauma is I can't stand being in really bright light. It invades my eyes and smothers me. Without shades it would be totally unmanageable. Ridiculous when I think I used to live in the glaring sunshine of Cyprus and Dubai. Now I'm happier in the shadows.

People entering the Thompson household are often shocked to find what appears to be a dominatrix's dungeon in the front room. They look through the door and see me bathed in red light with wires everywhere and a large mask attached to my head. Honestly, it's not what it seems. I'm not in a studded collar on the end of a dog lead. Thing is, while I'm between the red-light screens I'm also using thin air therapy, which entails me wearing breathing apparatus not dissimilar to an old World War Two gas mask. The idea is that breathing reduced-oxygen air encourages the development of new blood vessels. Widely used in sport by mimicking high-altitude training, tests have shown that it can increase energy as well as improve mood, memory and the ability to concentrate and perform everyday tasks.

I might soon be adding a pair of budgie smugglers to my wardrobe of unusual get-ups. Scientists have shown that cold water can produce a protein that slows the onset of dementia. Like anyone in a position where the stakes are so high, I am willing to try anything that offers a chance, even if crawling into a freezing cold lake in swimming trunks does make me fear slightly for the future of my testicles.

A little less likely to induce a public indecency charge is my use of CBD gels. CBD is found in cannabis plants but has nothing to do with the part that delivers a high. Potentially it can ease conditions including stress, inflammation, depression and anxiety – no wonder I have found it so incredibly helpful. Research is continuing to ascertain whether CBD can specifically help dementia patients by building connections between brain cells, aiding memory and other key functions. I'm no scientist but I can say I know more than a few people who swear by its healing abilities, friends who've been laid up with bad hips and are now back out on the course playing golf, for instance. It saddens me that I often see parents of young children with all kinds of conditions, including seizures, battling to get hold of CBD through the NHS. That child could drink five cans of fizzy sugary drinks a day and no one would bat an eyelid, but because people associate CBD with drugs it's virtually impossible for them to get something that would help them out massively.

As anyone living with a relative with dementia will know,

there are so many news stories about miracle cures that it's hard to know what's true, what offers genuine hope, and what's just been chucked out there for a quick headline. When I walk into the supermarket and see a paper screaming 'Experts Find Dementia Cure', I take it with a pinch of salt rather than allow it to get my hopes up. I've seen the same thing happen with cancer – constant stories about scientists being on the verge of a big breakthrough, and it never actually happens. However, where there is evidence to back up a treatment, I will, if possible, give it a try. Why wouldn't I? I have nothing to lose and everything to gain, as do those around me. The fitness, the treatment, everything I'm doing, is so Steph and the kids can have a more level me.

There are, though, some things that, science or no science, are against me. A good night's sleep is invaluable. It's when the brain does its sweeping up, clearing out the clutter, the toxins, the build-up of dangerous proteins that block blood flow and communication channels and sow the seeds of dementia within a brain with probable CTE. Put simply, it's what my brain needs to rest and reset. While I give myself a sleep score, measuring how good a night I've had against how many incidences of forgetfulness I have the following day, the fact I work at night can clearly affect my cognitive abilities, especially in the summer. Working nights in the winter isn't so bad because I get home in the dark. In the summer, the heat and the light make it virtually impossible to sleep. I get tired so quickly at times. Even cutting the hedge at the front of the house wears me out. We went round to a neighbour's house for a drink and one minute I was chatting away and the next I was asleep on Steph's shoulder. Literally mid-sentence.

I can be my own worst enemy. When it's a school day and everyone's up and about getting ready, I can't resist stumbling out of bed and being part of what's going on. There are times when I get just an hour's sleep. Those mornings are a nightmare; I'm so tired. But even if I'm not working, chances are I'll be lying awake at 4am panicking – *What's going to happen to me? To us? What am I going to do?* Sometimes I'll stare blankly at the ceiling wondering how long I actually have left, and then I'll feel one of the kids wriggling. Often they want to sleep in the bed with me. I love it, but sometimes I'm knackered and it's just not the right night. And then I look at them and think, *I can't tell them no – I need to enjoy every minute of this while I can.*

◈

When I first started addressing how I could respond to my diagnosis I felt frustrated at my lack of understanding of my brain's wiring. A little certainty about exactly what the future might look like would have been massive. Instead, all I had was confusion. I had images of my brain on my phone but what was the point when I didn't understand what the pictures were telling me? I didn't know if I was going to have a working brain for four years or twenty-four. Where was the cut-off point for recognising my family? Would I still be talking to them in 2025? Or would they be strangers to me?

The constant not knowing gnawed away at my insides. At a time when I needed as many truths as possible, the person who held out a hand was neuropsychiatrist John Ashcroft. From St Helens, John knew more than a bit about the physical demands of rugby and was well attuned as to how they could affect the brain. Previously, it felt like I'd been left in a void as various legal and insurance people got to grips with the case behind the scenes. But my brain damage is not something that I or Steph can just pack away and put to one side for a day in court. This is my, our, daily life, and so to speak to John and hear his views on what exactly the damage might mean was as deeply reassuring as it was helpful. The bad news was that, as ever, the minute we said goodbye I couldn't remember anything. The good news is we can record our meetings and I also have Steph's memory as a back-up. This is something we're going through together, so it's only right that she's there.

I kept jumping into the conversation on that initial call with John. Steph told me off for it, and she's right; in normal circumstances it would be really rude, but sometimes I feel I have to speak up because by the time there's a gap in the talking I'll have forgotten what I was going to say. John understood completely. It was as if he had a sixth sense as to how I was feeling. He instinctively knew the worries that were consuming me. I could speak about swings in my mental state and he was able to explain to me exactly what was going on in my brain to cause them. From the word go, it made such a difference to be working with someone who could not only help me to understand my condition but actually deliver constructive ways of how to address it. John reassured me that, while there can never be a definitive answer as to how I'll progress through the illness, there are reasons, mentally, psychologically and medically, why I should try to maintain a positive outlook. He reinforced in me that everyone's different. If two people break their leg, it's unlikely one will heal in exactly the same way as the other. When you see and hear dementia mentioned in general terms so much in the media, it's easy to forget there are a million different ways in which it can manifest itself. I needed to think of my case in the individual rather than the general.

John explained that now I'd been diagnosed and tested, there was a baseline from which to work. Beforehand I was operating blindfold. Was I getting worse quickly or slowly? At times it felt like both. One day I'd be feeling on top of my life, barely forgetting anything, tentatively thinking that it was all a bit of a fuss over nothing, the next I'd be out walking the dog, someone would ask me his breed and I wouldn't have a clue. It's a horrible thing to be constantly self-analysing, overthinking anything and everything, believing even the most insignificant of occurrences to be the top of a steep slide downwards into mental oblivion. Because those close to me also didn't have a clear understanding, I knew underneath that they were making all sorts of little assessments, too. Understandable – if you care about someone, you watch out for them, you want to know they're OK, check that they're not struggling, measure their decline.

As the 'patient', depending how you're feeling, that's either reassuring or depressing. Definitely, it can make you feel very self-conscious to know that your every word and action is being analysed and assessed. At its worst it can make you feel paranoid – that the minute you leave the room everyone is talking about you. You go from an individual in your own right to a 'person with dementia', entirely defined by the illness that is taking you over.

John, like all the excellent medical and psychiatric people I've encountered, knew that while of course I wanted hope, never did I want anyone to play down the situation. This isn't a TV show where one episode ends with a car careering towards a cliff edge and the next opens with its driver miraculously jumping clear with three feet of solid ground to spare. I can deal with the truth. What I can't deal with is the constant wondering. One thing I really don't need is doubt. While I couldn't appreciate others' love and concern more, I'm the one who lives in my head. Knowledge of what's happening to me and how my story might pan out is all that stops the mental torture; all that allows a little natural light into the cell in which I find myself trapped. A dementia diagnosis is a scar. Have no insight into what it means, and that scar will soon start to fester and become infected with fear, anxiety and that deep overwhelming guilt. To have no insight is massively psychologically damaging and causes great distress. That's why it's no good simply to diagnose someone with dementia and leave it at that. That person needs information and support. You can't tell them their mind is disintegrating and then expect them to go back to living their life like nothing has happened – 'You've got dementia – off you go!'

You can never be the same person before and after, and neither can those who share your life, which is why I fully expect at some point that counselling will become another source of help both to me and Steph. We might not entirely realise it, but I'm sure we're both carrying psychological damage from having this bombshell dropped on us. I look at Steph and think about how, overnight, the future she thought she had has been stripped away. I feel much more desperate for her than I do for myself. She's seen the worst of dementia in a way I never have. She lost her nan Kathy to the illness. This was a woman with a brilliant mind, a teacher at a big school, totally with it, a proper clever cookie. That's a terrible thing for anyone to see, and now Steph must face watching it happen all over again, this time to the man she loves and the father of her children. What does that do to someone? On the outside she's as strong as a rock, but that doesn't mean she's not wobbling inside. How can she not be when her world has been so violently turned upside down? I know myself from previous episodes of what now look very much like depression how easy it is to slip, barely noticing, into a different mental space. Her day-to-day is so busy, with all the incredible work she does for the family, it would be so easy for that to happen. I have heard it said also that a partner being diagnosed with dementia can essentially be the start of a grieving process. One way or another they are, at that moment, starting to say goodbye to the person they know. It makes me sick wondering what that long drawn-out farewell will be like for Steph, what it will do to her. If talking to someone helps to deflect that anguish, helps her navigate and make sense of this route that she has been dragged down, then I hope it will be made available to her and she will take it.

Having people around us who understand exactly what's going on has been massive. Expert opinion such as John's has allowed us to so much better comprehend the mechanics of what's happening inside my head, how over time concussion has caused connections to be compromised and sheared. I know now that the 'plasticity' of the brain allows it to adapt to its new state. That between each injury there may have been some degree of repair. Equally, the frequency of those injuries will have compromised the brain's ability to counter the damage, like a dumper truck of rubble arriving in your garden every few days while you try to clear it away with a bucket and spade.

John suggested that if I was to give my brain the best chance of longevity, I should give up the night shifts, but how can I? I can't just turn my back on one of the few remaining earning opportunities open to me. I know it's not healthy and I need my sleep. But who else is going to pay the bills? For me, it's an increasingly limited field of what I'm able to do. I enjoy my work, but hopefully at some point in the future I'll be able to earn a living and provide for my family during the day. I know also that there is the potential for drugs, not as a cure, but as a brake on the disease. John talked about medicines, sometimes designed for other conditions, that have been found to have benefits for brain injuries. Drugs that can lift me up, calm me down or put me on that plateau I so desire. With advice, I am more inclined to accept such an approach.

He also pointed out that, over time, as my self-awareness and understanding declines, the observations of those around me will become more and more important. Apparently, as the illness progresses, the gulf between how the patient perceives the situation and the reality of what their family sees becomes more and more extensive. The patient may think things are hunky-dory while those around them are living a different experience entirely.

More than anything, speaking to those with an understanding of my condition has confirmed that my future depends so much on doing anything and everything I can to slow the dementia down now.

My lifestyle choices today are more likely than anything to define my future. I know I'll start behaving in a different way and feel sick that I might be oblivious to such change. The hope is I can identify trends in my behaviour and have the ability to battle back against them. The hope is also that when people tell me I'm acting in a certain way, my illness doesn't immediately make me disbelieve them. It's that vanishing of awareness that scares me; that I should become a stubborn and intolerant presence in the house. That because of my dementia people will say, *It's not the real him, he can't help it*, while at the same time wishing they could have some respite from having to deal with me. Let me say right now, I am truly sorry if that happens. I don't want anyone ever to feel they *have* to be with me. If I am unbearable, put me away somewhere. Let me be that way out of sight and sound.

In the meantime, I'll work to maintain that competitive edge. If me and Seren are having a swimming race, I'll be there grabbing a leg, pushing her under – and she'll be doing exactly the same to me.

Seren, I'll keep giving you those fist bumps. Just don't tell Mum.

Chapter 14

MY STEVE
by Steph

When I heard Steve had dementia, my first thought was clear: *Oh my God. He's not got long. He's not going to watch the kids grow up. We're going to lose him*.

When you hear about any illness, the automatic reaction is to think the worst. But because of my nan I had good reason. The trauma was still fresh in my mind. At first we'd put the changes in her down to the confusion that comes with old age. She lived on her own and would do things like ask my mum to get her a pint of milk. Mum would call round, open the fridge door, and find ten bottles already there. Sounds daft, but even then we never twigged. We just thought she was a bit forgetful, or using the milk as an excuse for us to pop in. When she was then diagnosed with dementia we thought, *Of course, how did we not see it?*

And it was the same with Steve. When, finally, I saw his

behaviour as symptoms and not just him behaving a little bit oddly, it all made sense. Before that, even though he'd been struggling for a long time, I'd always put it down to something else – stress, tiredness, just generally getting older. That's why, when we first started talking to a specialist about the changes in Steve, I only mentioned the word 'dementia' in passing. 'Every now and again he reminds me of my nan,' I told her. 'I know it's not dementia. It can't be. But it does feel like that.' Little did I know.

I wasn't actually going to go on the trip to New Zealand where I met Steve because my mum and dad were over in Dubai on holiday, but they insisted – 'Go on, it'll be fun.' They were right. I first spotted him sat at a table in the hotel bar. We got talking and I noticed straight away his habit of talking with his hands – and how lovely those hands were. For his part, he noticed my Liverpudlian accent – something he's never quite let drop! I had no idea who he was and, I'll be honest, was devastated when I found out he was a sportsman. Bless them, but they don't really have the best reputation, do they? But Steve was so chatty and friendly that when he asked if I wanted to do something the next day, it didn't take me long to say yes. We've barely been apart since.

Three months after that first meeting, he proposed. He got a friend's little girl to do it. I was sitting next to her and noticed she was drawing wedding dresses – 'I want you to wear something like this on your wedding day,' she said. Then she asked me, 'Will you marry Steve?' I was a bit taken aback – 'Well, maybe one day.' And then she said it again. Only this time when I looked she had hold of a ring. I looked at Steve and he got down on one knee.

Within another three months we were married – in Las Vegas. Initially, we talked about doing the ceremony in fancy dress. I wanted him to dress as a bear. He won't thank me for saying it, but my nickname for him is 'teddy bear' – I could always see that, despite him being a pretty full-on character, there was a vulnerability underneath. I had another wish – that we be married by an Elvis lookalike. My nan loved Elvis.

On the day, we hopped into a cab to take us to one of Vegas's many 'just turn up' wedding venues. In the end we'd decided against the costumes, but it did so happen that the driver was the spit of Elvis – the hair, the face, everything except the rhinestone suit. He asked what we were up to and when we told him we were getting married he couldn't have been more excited. This was a man who absolutely loved weddings. He put us on the phone to his family – 'I've got these English guys in the cab, and you're never going to believe this . . .' He turned the meter off and drove us to this amazing wedding venue where we got married in front of a tumbling waterfall. On our honeymoon, we conceived our first baby. That might all sound a bit mad, but right from the start we just got each other. We both wanted the same thing and worked out that if we had a family early on then when they grew up we'd still have loads of years ahead of us to enjoy our lives together. Well, that was the plan.

I'm Steph and he's Steve, and so when I got pregnant he said he didn't mind what the baby was called – so long as the name began with 'S'.

'Right, OK,' I said. 'That doesn't restrict me at all!'

I thought of Seren, Welsh for 'star' – I've always had a thing about stars – and felt quite pleased with myself for coming up with something so lovely. I wasn't expecting to have to think of another three, but after no small amount of brain-racking, managed Slone, Saskia and Saxon. But there would be no more. The only 'S' Steve had to concern himself with now was the snip.

Eight years after Seren arrived, and two since Saxon, Steve now struggles to remember his children's names. Even the knowledge that they all begin with the letter 'S' isn't always enough to provide the mental trigger. Nor does he remember their births, even though he was present at them all, driving the nurses round the bend. With Seren I was in labour for almost twenty hours. I was in agony and he was stood there bouncing birthing balls off the walls. He was just a pest. With Saskia, he was hung-over and spent virtually the whole time in bed – my bed. 'Can I have the gas and air?' he kept asking the midwife. She just laughed at him. She'd been there for Seren, Slone and now Saskia. She knew him well enough. With Saxon, he didn't get a chance to lie down. It felt like I was in and out of the hospital in twenty minutes. On that occasion he appeared in a gown about three sizes too small, ripped open at several points. It was like being urged on by the Incredible Hulk. On each occasion, though, when the time came, Steve was the best, talking to me, stroking my face and calming me down.

At first when he was out of the game, Steve struggled. Being a sportsman provides a routine. They don't have to live in the real world. But having kids early on helped to get him used to a new and different kind of life. Dubai was lovely for toddlers, Steve was really successful with his work, and we made loads of friends. It was hard to imagine that anything could go wrong, but over time I began to notice changes in him, subtle at first, but gradually becoming more and more obvious. There would be massive outbursts of anger over really little things. Afterwards he'd apologise – 'I have no idea what that was about.' Neither did I, other than thinking I'd married a mard-arse, as us Liverpudlians say, or he was stressed by work, or tired from having little kids. One way or another, I'd always find an excuse for his behaviour. I saw it as his way of letting off steam. I knew he wasn't the sort of person to release the pressure by talking things through. Instead he'd bottle things up. That's what I was seeing in those early days – him just letting things build and build and then blow. He'd be OK for a while, and then I'd see it all bubbling up again until the inevitable eruption.

There was one thing I could definitely pinpoint as being a flashpoint. His temper would always fray if he had a social event on the horizon. Initially in Dubai, Steve enjoyed a busy social life, often out for drinks with the circle of friends he'd quickly made. But then after a while I began to notice a pattern. If he'd arranged to meet friends for a barbecue, or maybe there was a celebration or a party, the week before would be torture. Every time the same thing would happen.

'If it upsets you so much, stop making arrangements with people,' I'd say to him. 'What's the point if you don't enjoy it?'

'But I do enjoy it,' he'd reply. 'Once it's actually happening, I'm absolutely fine.' We still have that conversation now.

All the time I felt he was getting more and more forgetful. But early on he actually convinced me that I was the one with the problem. He was so adamant it was me who was mistaken that I'd be questioning my own actions. Being pregnant for a lot of the time in Dubai, I put it down to 'baby brain', the confusion and lack of concentration that can happen to women who are expecting. It was only when the kids got a bit older that I realised I'd been right all along. 'Daddy,' they'd say, 'it was you who forgot. You never told Mummy.' He wasn't trying to trick me. All that time his brain was telling him he was right.

Along with the forgetfulness, he became convinced that people, trusted friends and colleagues, were against him or didn't agree with the way he was working. I'd be emphasising that everything was fine, there was nothing going on, but he just couldn't see it.

'I don't think anybody likes me.'

'Of course they do. They're your mates.'

I was constantly telling him to calm down, stop being silly, that it was all in his mind – but it didn't work. If I pressed him on what the problem was, instead of telling me exactly what he was thinking he'd just claim it was something at work. 'I'm not talking to them,' he'd say. 'I don't want to be around them.' His headspace just didn't seem right and he began to talk about starting again somewhere else. Because Dubai was my home I didn't feel as ready to leave. But I could see the potential of another country for the kids. Dubai is so hot that you're stuck inside most of the time, and that's not great over a long period.

Initially when we moved to Cyprus, Steve mellowed out. But then came a phase where he just wouldn't come inside. All he'd do was sit outside all day. The kids would have to go out to see him. Looking back, we can see it was a spell of depression, but again, at the time we had no idea.

It was while we were in Cyprus that my nan passed away. I was pregnant with Saxon, too far gone to be able to fly over for the funeral. I felt awful. Nan meant so much to me and not to be there was dreadful. It was a moment that made me realise I had to go back to the UK. I missed my family too much. I've always had a close family set-up. At first Steve found that difficult to get used to – it was totally alien to his own experience. Now he loves it, and my mum and dad love him. They treat him like a son, although it still blows his mind that we speak to each other every night on the phone. 'What do you find to talk about!?' He wasn't raised like that, so I can see why he doesn't get it.

We set up home in the North West. With four little children you need all the help from family you can get and so it made sense. It felt like finally we were settling into some kind of rhythm, except there were still things happening with Steve that seemed odd. When he started forgetting the kids' names, it struck me as something your grandparents might do. They'd call you every name in their head before yours finally popped up. And then he started forgetting my name as well. 'Babe,' he'd say – and I knew he'd forgotten it.

'Babe?' I'd reply. 'What's my name?'

'I know your name,' he'd tell me – but he'd leave it at that.

It wasn't until Alix Popham rang that finally the jigsaw started coming together. Steve told me he was going to have tests to see if he'd suffered any long-term injuries while playing rugby. I looked at him. 'Of course you have, you doughnut. You can't move your arm. Your ankle's knackered.'

He didn't tell me he was talking about brain injury. He hoped it was nothing and didn't want to worry me. Only later when the tests actually started did he tell me what was really going on.

'I'm sure everything will be fine,' I told him. But I was scared – even more so when the results came back and there was that word – dementia. It was something neither of us ever expected to hear. Dementia? That's something you associate with old people. Steve was so young. It was as if our world had been flipped upside down.

At first we weren't going to tell the children. It's such a big thing. How do you get it across without frightening them? But when Steve came out in public about his problem, it was always going to be difficult to keep it from them. When the story appeared in the press, a lot of parents in the playground told me how sorry they were to hear the news. They were so kind, but Seren overheard a couple of things.

'What's wrong with Daddy?' she asked me.

I tried to brush it off – 'Oh nothing' – but she wasn't having it.

'No, something's wrong with Daddy.'

Back home, I told Steve, 'We're going to have to tell them. Otherwise they'll just hear stuff from somewhere else.'

We sat them down. 'Daddy's poorly in his head,' we told them.

'Like his body's poorly?' one of them asked.

'Well no, his head's a little bit more poorly than that. But don't worry about it,' we reassured them. 'People are just talking about it because it's in the newspapers.'

None of the kids understand Steve's behaviour to the depth we do. To them, a lot of the time it's funny. It makes them laugh when he does things like forget the dog's name, the name that he picked – Stan (another 'S' of course). 'Dad! Come on! It's Stan!' We love that a source of pain can also be a source of fun. We're like that with each other. We try to laugh it off.

There are, though, times where that's not so easy. I'll be honest, whenever he goes out, I'm terrified. He has times when he'll just completely forget everything. In the back of my head I'm thinking, *What happens if he completely forgets where he is or gets lost?* It happens. He was driving to visit a friend recently and completely forgot where he was going.

He called me.

'What am I doing?'

'You're in the car.'

'Yes, but what am I doing?'

'You're going to meet a friend.'

'Oh. Where?'

'Costa.'

'Right – which one?'

'The town centre.'

'I don't know how to get there.'

You do know. You've been there loads of times.

'Just put it in the satnav and go off that.'

'Oh, right. OK.'

He put the phone down, and all I could think for the rest of the morning was, *Is he OK? Has he got there all right? Has his trail of thought gone again? Has he just driven off into the middle of nowhere?* Little things like that are in my head all the time. If he takes the kids to school, I'm thinking, *I hope he doesn't switch off and take them to the park instead.* I don't want him ringing me two hours later from the seafront at Blackpool!

He knows I worry and so calls and messages all the time. If he's just down the road somewhere I know also that if he has a panic attack I can get to him quickly. It's when he's away that I really start to worry. What if something happens to him then? Recently he did a long-distance bike ride with friends and I was terrified the whole way through. Obviously, he couldn't message to say he was OK while he was riding.

If I can't be with him, it stresses me out. But at the same

time I want him to live his life. I say that to him: 'You've got to find joy in life. You've got to do these things.' Because, ultimately, his happiness is everything. If he sits at home and thinks about what's going to happen, then the situation will just swallow him up. It's important that he maintains friends, not just so he can relax but so he can unburden himself of the things he can't or won't say to me. The last thing I want is him keeping things in, the pressure building and building.

At the same time, it's massive to me that we face this situation together, even if sometimes it's far from easy. Steve asked me to watch the Will Smith film *Concussion* about mass brain injury in the NFL. In all honesty, I didn't want to. I thought something like that – the blunt reality of head trauma in sport and its potential aftermath – would be too much. 'I think you should,' he said, 'just in case.' So I did – and it scared me. There was a lot of stuff about suicide which I found really hard to watch, because Steve himself talks to me about how hard it is to go on. He has massive downs. A few weeks ago, he was on the floor emotionally, completely broken down, in floods of tears, head in hands. At times like that he'll talk about how exhausted he is, how it would be better for everyone if he wasn't here, how he feels like giving in to his darker thoughts. I know he wouldn't – I'd batter him if he did! – but my heart's in my mouth every time he goes off fishing. When Steve's down in that pit, I say to him, 'Look at your kids. They're what you've got to live for. Look at them.'

I know he tries to keep his emotions in check because he

doesn't want to upset me. I don't want to upset him either and so I cry on all my mates. It's like a pipe has burst. I try to be strong. But it's hard. I just feel so sad for him. All this for a sport – for a game of bloody rugby.

Yes, I get angry. When the diagnosis came through, my first reaction was disbelief – *It can't be – it's definitely not that.* Then came the hurt and the upset. And then the anger at what's happened to him – for the result of playing a game to be someone eventually forgetting who their children are. I can accept physical injuries. We both knew he was bashed and bruised. His body is so smashed up from rugby that last year he couldn't move one of his arms. At times he couldn't get up off the sofa and I'd have to help lift him up. He would struggle to walk up the stairs and so I'd walk behind him to make sure he didn't fall. I used to joke with him: 'Next house we'll definitely need a downstairs bedroom and bathroom – or a Stannah stairlift.'

'I'm not pushing a pram and a wheelchair at the same time!' I used to tell him. 'I haven't got that many arms!' Now those things don't seem quite so funny. It's as if his physical injuries were giving me an insight into dementia. He was just so poorly, as if his body had given up. It was heartbreaking to see someone his age in such a state.

When we had Saxon, people would sometimes ask, 'Is he going to play rugby?'

'You've got to be joking,' I'd say. 'Have you seen the state of Steve? Not a chance.' And that was before we even knew what had happened to his brain.

Thankfully, we are both very proactive in repelling the effects of dementia. Steve's illness will never get better but, if all goes to plan, me and the kids can have him with us longer than I initially thought. I said to him from the start, 'We're going to do anything we can to help you.' And we have. He's so much healthier now. He keeps himself fit, eats well, does all the recommended treatments. The kids have become part of that too. They help fill his bucket up for the icepacks he uses morning and evening to ease the pain and swelling on his ankles, feet, knees, elbows and hands.

I hope also he'll get help to deal with his darker thoughts. As it stands, he's pretty much had the diagnosis and that's it. I spoke to him about seeing someone and his view was, 'Don't worry – we'll fix this together. We'll sort it.' But I couldn't accept that.

'We're not going to fix it. This is permanent. We need help.'

This is the day-to-day situation with dementia that people on the outside don't see: the way it invades every basic element of life, the way it twists and distorts emotions. Steve feels guilty. As a dad, he's supposed to care for his kids – and now he sees that potentially being the other way round. He's a proud man – imagine how that makes him feel.

There's another thing he says – that I never signed up for this. But he's wrong. This is exactly what I did sign up for. I love the bones of him. I'd do anything for him and when the time comes I will do everything I can to look after him. He can't feel guilty for something that's completely out of his control. Anything can happen in life, and when you're married you look after someone as much as you can for as long as you can.

My main focus has to be making sure Steve's healthy and happy because, if that's the case, that feeling of normality follows. We're lucky that as a family we're all at our happiest when we're together. Steve loves being around the kids, and we all love being around him. Forget the man people used to see on the rugby pitch; he's a big softie really. He's not as hard to mollycoddle as people might think. His dream day is making pancakes in the morning and then sitting on the sofa watching films with the kids. It all feels so normal that it's hard to imagine there's something lurking underneath.

The temptation is to shut the door on the outside world and try to preserve those normal family days forever, but at the same time Steve is determined to fight for our future – and the futures of others – which is why he went public with his diagnosis. Sadly, the trolls and keyboard warriors are everywhere and people couldn't wait to pile in when the link was made between rugby and his dementia. 'He's just after the money.' 'I didn't hear him complaining at the time.' 'He's trying to ruin the game.' My husband is a human being. How people can write stuff like that is beyond me. I try to close my eyes to it, but Steve is there in front of me. I see what the game has done to him. Anyone who thinks this is about money should walk a few hundred yards in his shoes.

Our future is living day-to-day. I don't want to look for

issues – the situation is scary enough as it is – I'd rather just tackle them as they happen, trying to make sure we're all OK. I'd like to think that for a good time yet we can carry on doing what we've always enjoyed, be it holidays, days out, whatever. At the same time, it's impossible not to notice even the slightest changes in Steve's character. Recently, it's felt like he's got amnesia. A conversation or a story will come in pieces. He'll forget, then he'll remember, then he'll forget again. The freshness of what can go can be a shock. We were watching a TV drama and he just couldn't get his head round this particular scene – 'Hang on, what's happened to him?'

'He's died. We just saw it happen.'

We had to rewind the programme so he could watch it again. 'I don't remember seeing that.' I was sitting there thinking, *How can something go that quickly?*

I've seen the same happen with the dog. He'll be telling me 'Stan did this, Stan did that,' and then within a second the name has gone.

Other things, though, are definitely more reminiscent of dementia. Steve can remember stuff from being a little kid, but when I see him talking rugby memories with a friend I know exactly what's going on – he's convincing himself that he remembers whatever anecdote has been mentioned. Later, I'll say, 'I could tell you didn't remember.' And he'll admit it. 'I didn't have the faintest idea what they were on about.'

What really brings the state of his brain home is when he watches clips of his rugby career and can't remember even being on the pitch. The first few times I saw it happen I'd think, *How can you not remember when you can actually see yourself running up and down on the screen?* It must be so odd to look at yourself as a stranger. We came across a promotional video he did in Dubai for HSBC.

'Do you remember that?' I asked.

'No, not at all.' And I'm thinking, *But it wasn't that long ago!*

When he started forgetting the kids' names it was particularly upsetting. I wasn't so bothered about me. You don't think so much about yourself once you've had kids. I'll take anything – wife, whatever! But with the kids it made me start thinking about the long term – how my nan went and how she didn't remember my mum, or any of us. When I think about that, it's so hard not to get upset. You know what's ahead, don't you?

Sometimes it feels like everything we do is a tap on the shoulder of what's coming down the line. We recently bought our forever house, one of those places in which you can see yourself growing old with the person you love. Immediately, I had visions of the two of us opening the front door to grandkids; them running around everywhere. And then I was brought up short. *Maybe it won't be the two of us.* It's hard to write those words through the tears. I can only console myself that, if the worst does happen, Steve will be looking down on it all unfolding beneath him, knowing he will always be a massive part of whatever's going on.

All we can do is keep going – keep hoping that day will

never come. Like Steve always says, he's got me and the kids and that's what keeps him going. Together we can and will take on anything that gets in our way. We've overcome so much to get this far, so we know we have that inner strength. We just want to enjoy our lives together for as long as we can. Our little pack.

We know also that, for some families, sadly, that's an impossibility. Time together is something they can never get back.

Chapter 15

THE LOST CHILD

Ben Robinson was fourteen. On 29 January 2011, as I looked forward to England's opening Six Nations encounter against Wales, this 'vibrant, awesome and loving' (his dad Peter's words) youngster was playing a game of rugby for his school. As the second half neared its end, he slumped to the floor. Mum Karen ran on to the pitch. She held his arm and put him in the recovery position. It was too late. She could only watch as he slipped away.

Ben had been concussed earlier in the game. Karen could see he was in a bad way. She'd spent most of the game agonising about his condition, bemused and despairing that, despite her son staggering around and showing clear signs of confusion, other than the old standby of sticking a few fingers up in front of his face and asking him to count them, no one took any action. Ben died not because of a tragic accident or an incurable illness; he died because he played rugby. I feel so many emotions when I read about Ben, and anger is right up there among them. Rugby could have prevented Ben's death. It could have accepted the clear risks that the game presented – knowledge that was well established at that time – and acted. Had it done so, Ben would be alive. I hate saying that, because for Ben's family it's just another reminder of how needless it was for him to die. But the truth is that information about the potentially devastating effects of concussion was widely available. Protocols could and should have been in place to make sure a child showing clear signs of concussion was removed from the pitch and immediately examined. Instead, concussion regulation was loose and muddled, not well delivered, and open to individual interpretation. The end result was that the necessary action to save Ben wasn't taken.

It sticks in my throat a little that, while in the ten years since Ben died so little action was taken, as soon as ex-professional rugby players like myself started talking about brain injury and the need for change, suddenly – Boom! – the game began to take notice. What about all those who came before? Did they not matter? Were they not important? It's things like that which form the basis of my drive for change, because I cannot stand to see that injustice; cannot stand to see people pushed to one side and forgotten; cannot stand to see how badly families have been treated.

I feel guilty that Ben is no longer with us. I shouldn't, because at that time I didn't know any different. I didn't know rugby could be lethal. But I do sometimes wonder if I could have identified my own issues earlier. Who knows? Had I done so, Ben might still be alive. Instead of doing it now, I could have been putting pressure on the Rugby Football Union (RFU), the sport's governing body in England, to make protocols more stringent a decade ago. As it is, I hope Ben's name will always be a driving factor in ensuring the game is as safe as possible for generations of young people to come. Sadly, I'm not so confident. It is, after all, several thousand days since Ben died. How, after all that time, can the discussion over concussion still be alive?

I'm incredulous when I see how slow the game is to learn and implement lessons. There are people in rugby, from top to bottom, who remain oblivious to the risks, see protocols as an inconvenience, or just don't take concussion seriously. Even as I'm writing, I'm looking at a clip of England and Exeter Chiefs hooker Luke Cowan-Dickie lying flat out after taking a massive bang to the head in a tackle during the Premiership Grand Final at Twickenham. Next day, Luke was on the plane for the Lions tour of South Africa. By the Thursday he was contact training. A week after that horrific impact he came off the bench and was back playing. The management said they had followed all the protocols. Fine, except any protocol which says a concussed player can be back on the pitch in a week is wrong. Plain wrong. It flies in the face of widespread and accepted knowledge that the correct period of rest should be at least thirty days. Even in the eighties, it was three weeks. But instead of making concussion protocols stricter, in 2011, global governing body World Rugby, then the International Rugby Board, reduced the minimum time a professional player should be sidelined from three weeks to as little as six days. That's deep into the professional era when players are bigger and faster than ever. In terms of making sense, it's like being caught in a downpour and putting down your umbrella. If a player comes back too soon there is the risk that the brain isn't working at its optimum, which compromises their decision-making and increases the risk of another concussion. If a player has a muscle injury or their cruciate ligament goes, they aren't rushed back. Just because an injury isn't visible doesn't mean it's any different.

The problem is that the people making the decisions around safety in sport have skin in the game. Professional sport is paid for by revenue, and the dominant view is that doing something radical might threaten that income and put the organisation at risk. The way sport is set up, there's very little incentive to do what's right for the players. It's business, and money talks. Maybe it isn't too cynical to wonder if reducing the rest period to a week has more to do with keeping star players on TV, which puts so much revenue into the game, and less to do with safe concussion protocols. Do the broadcasters keep pumping in the money if the best players aren't going to be out there to attract the viewing figures that in turn satisfy the advertisers?

Somewhere in that wheel of business, the big bucks, the pound signs, it seems like player welfare – the most important element by far – has been lost. There are some who see the choice facing rugby as one between radical change and squeezing out profit. That's actually not a choice, it's basic morality. And yet all too often sports tend to delay and not do the right thing. Leadership should come from the top. The highest echelons of the game should be setting an example to every other tier. Do the right thing and others will follow. That way, the next time a situation such as Ben's occurs there will be no questioning, no prevaricating, no waving fingers in front of eyes. The player will be straight off.

I don't see how anyone can argue with updating the protocols of rugby union. But still they do. When it was revealed I was fighting for change in the game, I received endless messages – 'You're ruining my son's life,' 'I've lost all respect for you.' I don't know how many times I can say it: myself and others who have gone down this route are not seeking to destroy the game. We want people to play rugby. But we also want an obvious element of risk to be recognised and eradicated. It's not like rugby hasn't adapted before. In the old days, when someone was on the floor, you'd be able to ruck them out. That was stopped because it was dangerous – players could get raked or trodden on. To most people, that was a sensible move. But there were some, as ever, up in arms – 'They're making the game soft.' No, they're making it safer!

Sports adapt – they always have and they always will – and often for the better. Some football coaches complain about kids not being allowed to head the ball in training any more. But take a look at five-a-side. The ball isn't allowed to go above shoulder height and people love it. Rugby league got rid of shoulder charges and spear tackling. Stadiums are still packed out.

If a sport is good enough in the first place, it will adapt and survive. When Australia's cricketers were hit repeatedly on the head and upper body during the infamous Bodyline Ashes series of 1932–33, the rules were changed to banish the tactic. After the death of Ayrton Senna in 1994, Formula 1 revamped tracks, added more race-day medical staff, and cockpits were reworked to prevent drivers becoming trapped. Following the death of a rider in the Paris–Nice stage race in 2003, pro cycling made helmet wearing compulsory. In other words, sports have been adapting for decades. Times change, as does body shape, athleticism and technology. You can't just say, 'It's part of the sport,' and leave it there. That's not good enough. Worse, it's downright irresponsible.

I have zero time for those who say, 'We played hard in my day and it never did me any harm.' How do you know? They tend to be the same people who state, 'Toughening up kids is what rugby is all about.' I used to play around in abandoned buildings – doesn't mean I want my kids to do the same. The whole 'toughening up kids' standpoint is so misplaced. For a start, that really isn't what rugby is all about – it's about fun. Secondly, when medical evidence exists that elements of a sport are causing significant risk to the brain, how does 'toughening up kids' fit into its justification? Remember when the adverts used to say smoking was good for you? And then everyone had lung cancer? Would it have been better if we'd pretended that link wasn't there? Hiding behind silly macho attitudes doesn't make problems go away – it kills people.

Such people, as Twitter has made abundantly clear, genuinely think what I'm doing is wrong; that the hits, the bangs, the crashing impacts and broken bones are all part of what makes the game so character-forming. It disturbs me massively that some of those people are junior coaches. Thankfully, they are in a minority and there are many more coaches out there who see the welfare of young people in their charge as their overriding concern. They can see that the game isn't going soft, it's going safe; that if something is dangerous, then it has to be addressed. A parent doesn't expect their child to be put in danger in a rugby environment any more than they expect a Scout leader to take them playing on a railway track.

Forget, 'If you get rid of that element it won't be the same'. What matters more? Safety? Players? A devastated parent? Or that a spectator feels a little bit disappointed while they sip their Bovril on the sidelines? Anyone who loves rugby or plays the game should be driving for change, because change is not what will destroy the sport: it's what will save it. I've seen columns in newspapers where ex-players, some of them former England colleagues of mine, say, 'The sport gave me so much. I'm not going to get involved in knocking it.' They're just happy, they say, to have had the career they've had. I'd like to ask them a question. If someone came up to you and said, 'You're going to play rugby for England and you're going to win the World Cup, but you won't be able to remember it, you won't be able to work, and you won't be able to provide for your kids,' would you take that?

I've got a follow-up. If the price of your son or daughter playing rugby was the loss of their mental faculties, would you still talk in such a blasé manner? Great, rugby worked for you. But it's a very simplistic, potentially cowardly attitude to then turn away, to go back to your wine cellar and your after-dinner speeches. What about those who have been left struggling? What about those who come after you? Do you not see that by sticking our heads above the parapet, ex-players like me are trying to make the game safer for future generations? Rugby will always, one way or another, be a contact sport, but we owe it to those following in our footsteps to make it safer. Action needs to be taken now. Otherwise, thousands more will end up like me. I can't carry on like nothing has happened, because rugby is slowly stripping me of my dignity and turning me into an empty shell. And even if that wasn't the case and it was happening to someone else, I'd like to think I would still have the ability to see that the game was at fault, that people were becoming ill and dying, and there was a critical need for change. I'd like to think I would show a bit of empathy. I'd like to think I'd get up off my arse and do something.

In any dire situation, someone has to stand up and drive change or else nothing will ever happen. When it comes to brain damage, I'm happy not to be lying on a beach waiting for someone else to take hold of the reins. You can't do that when it's so obvious that a change of course is so desperately needed. But what's needed more than anything is for rugby to seize its own chance to be proactive. For its own future it has to act. If it doesn't, more and more people of all ages and sexes will walk away from the game. Already we are seeing players reacting to the dementia crisis by quitting in their twenties. Who can blame them? They have gone through the pros and cons and concluded there's no point playing a sport that could put them in a nursing home. Sport is something most people do to stay healthy, not have their future snatched away.

Evidence shows that, until the rugby authorities face up to wholesale regulation changes, those who walk away are making a wise choice. When almost three million people's medical records were analysed by researchers in Denmark and the USA, the results were shocking – a serious concussion in your twenties means a two-thirds increase in the risk of being afflicted by dementia in the following thirty years. Elsewhere, parents are making the choice for their children. When they switch on the radio and hear that the younger a person when sustaining a head injury, the higher the risk of developing dementia, they're more than entitled to drive straight out of the rugby club car park and never go back. No sport wants to be losing a large number of kids – essentially its future – because parents are being scared off. But what parent could ever be blamed for keeping their child away from rugby while there's an avoidable risk of them being concussed?

Plummeting participation numbers and concerned parents

mean no longer can rugby's hierarchy dismiss the potentially devastating consequences for their sport. You need only look at the report by the Drake Foundation, a non-profit organisation dedicated to researching concussion in sport, to see that the game is at a crossroads. Take the wrong turn now and it faces oblivion. The foundation's survey found that 66 per cent of parents whose children play rugby want scrums to be banned from youth rugby and 69 per cent want physical contact in training to be limited. Some 65 per cent want tackling to be banned from Under-14 rugby and more than one in two want it banned from Under-16 and Under-18. The number of parents concerned that playing rugby could have a long-term effect on their child's health stands at 58 per cent. At amateur level, the survey reports, 64 per cent of those who play regularly for an organised team are 'very' or 'somewhat' concerned that playing could have an adverse effect on their long-term health, while 63 per cent have decided to limit the amount they play or give up playing completely. At elite level, the Drake Foundation scanned 44 players. The results were startling – 23 per cent had abnormalities in brain structure, specifically in blood vessels and the white matter which, with its neural pathways, is so crucial to our cognitive ability. In a time when people have endless leisure alternatives, those are not great numbers for any sport seeking to cement its future.

Rugby needs to start over. With the young, it especially needs to lose the bad habits it's picked up from the repositioning of the adult game. Why is it that even at junior level we're setting kids up to smash each other? Looking back to their childhoods, people in their forties and fifties will remember rugby as a sport of running. In the old days, kids would be out on the pitch, round the ball like bees round honey, only doing a couple of tackles a game. Nowadays they're organised in defensive lines, regimented – 'Do this! Do that!' When did collision become everything in rugby? People used to talk about a player's ability to run with the ball, their handling skills. The game has been turned into the playground game of bulldog – on steroids. The joy of the game at that young age, the haring about, the skill of beating an opponent, has gone. It's all about systems, power, running into each other. And that's all the way down. I look at that and can't help thinking, *When did rugby just become that? When did it become so one-dimensional and boring?* If, as a parent, I took my son or daughter to play, I know what I'd be thinking: *Is there not a club where they can just kick the ball around?*

I've been to clubs and watched hour-long coaching sessions where the kids have played for ten minutes. The rest of the time was used up discussing tactics. The most important thing in any session is that kids get to play and enjoy the game. If they're standing around all the time, they're soon going to get bored and look elsewhere for entertainment. Ultimately, that child is then lost to the sport. Often such coaches obsess over winning rather than giving everyone a go. Coaches who operate like that are effectively running those sessions for their own ego. Rugby needs to look at the bigger picture of what it is and what it needs to be. In the modern world, more than anything it needs to be something that gets kids out from in front of their computers and helps in the fight against obesity. That won't happen if parents are concerned about the game's safety and those kids who do go along just think it's tedious. Kids of all shapes and sizes can enjoy touch rugby. It's a running game which is fun, exciting and keeps everyone interested. In a world with so many distractions, if a sport doesn't engage with new generations, then it's dead on its feet.

People argue that it's wrong to stop contact rugby for young kids because they need to learn at an early age. Do they? In a few years' time, when the sport has changed, they'll know about evasion techniques instead. They'll play the game in a different way. When they get older and want to progress, you then make sure that all the protocols are there to ensure it's as safe as possible to do so. No way would I want any of my children to play rugby the way it is at the moment. I wouldn't want them to be storing up issues for the future and I wouldn't want them to be facing the immediate risks of impact. With young kids whose brains are still growing, you have to take out the tackle and the rucks. On any level, it cannot be good for a developing brain to be subjected to constant unnecessary knocks and collisions.

One tragedy should be enough to make a sport leap to action. But rugby has responded with disinterest and delay. Can the sport honestly tell parents it is doing everything in its sway to keep their children safe? While it drags its feet over the issue of young people playing contact rugby, it can never make that claim. A well-run, responsive and responsible sport adapts with the times. Why should anyone else go through the hurt that Ben Robinson's family has suffered? Addressing rugby's issues isn't some wishy-washy concept. Nor is it just about dementia. It's about young people suffering catastrophic injuries that can change their lives. Or end them. The sport needs to give direction and leadership as to whether contact rugby should be removed from the school curriculum. Schools also need to bite the bullet and make that decision. There can't be any argument that outweighs the safety of children. What the hell kind of world are we living in when children face potentially life-changing, even fatal, head trauma and the response is to sit back and say, 'Well, that's rugby – that's just how it is,' and do nothing?

When people on Twitter tell me I want to destroy rugby, they couldn't be more wrong. What I actually want to do is ensure it is safe so there's not another Ben. How can anyone who loves rugby look that young boy's parents in the face and tell them we don't owe them that?

Chapter 16

SMASHED

When you're young, you think the people who run sport are looking out for you. Slowly you start to understand they are actually looking out for themselves. By then it's too late.

It moves and upsets me to think that Ben Robinson's life was so short as to span my career as a professional rugby player. It makes me think also about how the game changed during that time. How players became crash-test dummies, and how what starts at the top of a sport always filters down through the levels.

As I've said, when rugby bit the bullet and went professional, the sport quickly became more and more strength-based. As the first through the door, we were the ones taking the punishment. 'Defence wins matches,' seemed to be all I ever heard as rugby went from a free-flowing game to one based on collision. Don't just take my word for it. Have a look on YouTube at the comparison between the open running game of the decades pre-professionalism, and the smash, crunch and grind that followed. Faster, heavier, stronger – that's all that mattered. I myself went from someone with real agility, running around the pitch, really enjoying the game, to a solid block with a 24-inch neck. Bearing in mind the average UK male's waist size is 37 inches, you can see that I was basically half man, half bull.

To feed the game's desire for power, a massive gym culture sprang up, which I neither liked nor felt particularly suited me. I have what I call 'farmer strength' – get me wrestling and there ares not many who can beat me. But make me do bench presses and it's never going to be the same. I could barely reach 150 kg while some England players would be doing way bigger numbers. Where I did come into my own was the deadlift. With all the power in my legs and arse, I could do more than 300 kg. Farmer, you see – I'd have been great at shifting bales. And, like a farmer, I never seemed to have a day off.

There was so little respite. Win the World Cup and barely had we touched down at Heathrow than we were back in training with our clubs. Even after reaching the final of Euro 2020, well into July, England's footballers had a few weeks on the beach before reporting back, but between 2001 and 2007, aside from missing a two-Test tour of Australia in June 2006, I played pretty much relentlessly, summer and winter. All I did, week after week, was play rugby, being smashed again and again. With any gaps in the club calendar filled with internationals, my body was just hanging together, which made the fact I'd never suffered a serious injury up to that point even more remarkable. I'd pick up knocks, but not serious enough to stop me either training or playing. I'd always be on the team sheet; always on the training pitch. The coaching staff would just strap me up and throw me back in. That meant I was playing forty games a season. My head and body were being put through continual hammering.

None of that mattered to anyone, though. Whatever the demands put on me physically, I knew what was being said among the hierarchy – 'It's Wally, he'll do it. It'll be fine.' That message became ingrained in my head after a while and I started to believe I was somehow unbreakable. Even if I did suffer an injury, rest was never the option. One time, I damaged the medial ligament in my knee. It was strapped up and back on to the pitch I went. Other times I'd lift a shoulder and the pain would be unbearable. The solution? Painkillers, jabs. Never recuperation. If injury to the body is treated as an inconvenience, something to be patched up, then is it any wonder that head injury was, and, in some quarters still is, not treated any differently?

It wasn't just me. I would see my fellow crash-test dummies knocked out, stagger around for a bit, and still be kept on the pitch. And in all honesty that player might have pushed for that decision. They might have wanted to stay on to help the team, or maybe just to look tough. Teammates too, desperate not to lose an influential colleague, might also urge a coach to keep them on. This was the dynamic of the sport. Walking off a rugby pitch because you felt a bit woozy was a sure-fire way of being branded a 'pussy'. In fact, someone being poleaxed, staggering around trying to find their balance, often gave everyone a laugh, a bit like in cricket when a batsman gets hit in the balls. In rugby, ignorance was the victor while common sense was red-carded and sent to the back of the stand. *The game – all that matters is the game –* it's an illusion that takes over the mind.

I've suffered cuts around my eyes from flailing fingernails, run off to be stitched, gone straight back on, and then been restitched properly after the game. Imagine that in any other walk of life. Imagine that in a factory. You crush a finger in a machine, stick a plaster on, and then nip down to the hospital at home time. Thing is, carrying on was all that mattered. I was blind to any other option. *Just let me get through to half-time and I'll be all right.* In exactly the same way, I was known for taking a knock, spending ten seconds in the land of the fairies, and then cracking on like nothing had happened. But something quite obviously had. My brain had been violently jolted. Think about braking suddenly in your car and what happens to that takeaway coffee in the drinks' holder by the gearstick, how it sloshes all over the place. My brain wanted to do the same, but it had nowhere to go. All it could do was smash against my skull on one side and then recoil back against the other, the intensity of that impact ricocheting backwards and forwards in its ever-rotting core.

This mix of competitive desire and lack of deep medical

understanding means a decision on fitness to continue after a head injury can never be taken by those invested in the game. Players are blinded by loyalty to the cause, competitive desire, a fear of looking weak and losing their place. Coaches, often under pressure, just want to win. In that case, the only opinion that can be deemed safe is a medical or welfare officer. None of us does our own driving test and decides whether we're safe enough to go on the roads. What's the difference with impacts and people playing rugby?

I know for a fact my brain was routinely mashed during games. Many a time a teammate would talk to me afterwards, bringing up a certain incident or decision, and I'd be sitting there totally blank.

'When the referee penalised that scrum,' they'd say, 'I thought we wouldn't get another chance.' *What scrum? What the hell are you on about?* And for years I thought I was normal. They were the weird ones. In a full-on game, how could anyone but a complete oddball recall such detail? You forget things. It's what people do. Except they don't – at least not at my age, not like me. It was me who was odd. Instead of images of the last frenetic eighty minutes, I had tumbleweed drifting across the wasteland of my mind.

Thankfully, there are players now who will actually alert the coaching staff if they see a player has taken a knock. That's a victory, but the issue is about a lot more than just what happens on the pitch. Like any professional I was training relentlessly. As an amateur, I'd train twice a week. As a pro, it was often twice a day. Even if I was carrying an injury, the message was the same: 'If you don't train, you don't play.' With England especially, where game time is clearly more limited, and competition for places intense, sometimes the only way to prove yourself is in training. That never lets up. Even when you're the man in possession, you still have to battle hard. Take your foot off the pedal and immediately there'll be someone in the rear-view ready to barge you out of the way. That fear of missing out is exactly why I accepted being pushed down a certain route in terms of power and size. If being bigger and stronger was deemed to be required, then were I to continue to be effective, not to mention selected, I had to buy into that ethos. You can't just be a professional on a Saturday. To reach the top and stay there you have to work hard day in, day out to be what your club or country wants you to be. For a hooker like me that meant knocks to the head were a daily occurrence. Time and again I'd be knocked out in training and, again, the level of concern from those around me would be nothing more than a shrug of shoulders. After all, it was just Thommo, and Thommo was always OK – wasn't he?

No one would give it a second thought. No one was saying, 'Hang on, you'd better sit out the rest of the session while we get you assessed.' Players were being totally bulldozered and would just haul themselves back to their feet and carry on. Five minutes later the same thing might happen all over again. Imagine driving your car into a wall, getting back in, and repeating it over and over. You'd have to be mad. But in rugby there seemed to be a feeling that getting smacked on the head every day was a good way to practise the game. In France, training was especially prehistoric. In England, coaches would lay off the hardcore training the day before a game, but in France we'd be doing full contact sessions. I tried to educate them, but it was pointless. It was part of their rugby culture. They had to be full-on all the time.

Wherever I played, more times than I'd care to remember even if I could, I would be told to pit my solid, eighteen-stone self against the near immovable force that was a scrum machine. Believe me, piling into one of those things is nobody's idea of fun. You have your own momentum, plus that of the back row, forcing you into a piece of equipment that looks like it should be on a farm not a sports field. Sometimes to make it tougher, to increase the resistance, other players would stand on the frame. Essentially, you were being crushed against it, everything coming through your shoulders, neck and head. I would actually begin to feel myself passing out. When, finally, we released, I would have little white dots floating before my eyes – like the stars that cartoon characters see when they get an anvil on the head. It would be a few seconds before I knew what the hell was going on again. But this was how hard we were worked. Losing your senses became just one of those things. Slamming into a scrum machine was my daily routine just the same as someone else's might be working at a laptop or driving a van. It genuinely felt like coaches couldn't think of anything else for us forwards to do. After all, they had gone from two nights a week to full-time like the rest of us.

How were they supposed to fill those endless hours? Other times they'd lay off the scrum machine and have us smash into each other instead. One day we practised the scrum a hundred times. A ton of men battering into one another. A hundred times! They might as well have rung the army and had us ram a tank. So much about that kind of training doesn't make sense. You are basically asking players to reach peak fitness while constantly knocking seven shades of shit out of them – on top of whatever happens on the pitch. I don't think any rugby player can ever say they are one hundred per cent fit. If concussion protocols are introduced, and the impacts are reduced, maybe that's a claim a player will finally be able to make.

My natural competitiveness meant I wouldn't hold back in training any more than I would on the pitch. Thing is, in pro-sport, make a fuss, take a stand, and you risk being dropped. That's not just your name on the team sheet gone, it's your future and livelihood. My job, it was crystal clear, was to have the shit knocked out of me. And if that was my job, how could I complain about it? It's like a baker complaining about the smell of bread. A steeplejack about heights.

By the end of my career, it felt like the bulldog training ethos was beginning to fade a little. Training became more scientific. Coaches seemed to overcome their communal amnesia and remember that technical skills can also win games. I'm not saying they were looking for a wholesale shift back to the heady days of Gareth Edwards sprinting sixty yards to score perhaps the greatest try of all time for the Barbarians against the All Blacks in 1973, but I know for sure the World Cup build-up I experienced in 2011 was some way removed from the full-on physical onslaught of my earlier years, the endless merry-go-round of playing and training which meant I was going through the equivalent of dozens of controlled car crashes every day.

Training these days tends to be more targeted, with players working towards individual as well as collective goals, rather than the constant physical contact with either each other or equipment that I saw. For me, though, the pullback from sledgehammer rugby came ten years too late. The result of that daily punishment is there's a great slab of my life that quite literally no longer exists. The middle bit – peak rugby-playing me – is gone. You don't need to be a genius to work that one out. That mid-section is when the bulk of the damage was done. Also, the fact I saw some progress towards the end of my career doesn't mean there was an unveiling of a great new era of safety for the game. The RFU's own figures show that in 2018–19, for the eighth consecutive season, concussion was the most common professional match injury, standing at 20 per cent of all those reported. Those figures show that in the same year, there were 166 match concussions and thirty-eight training concussions. Almost one in five concussions occurred in training.

Collision, often at speed, remains a massive part of a team's armoury. Just look at the back-up power some teams have on the bench – big units specifically there to come on towards the end of the game and impose themselves on tired opponents.

It's got to the point where a team might actually start with a weaker player in a certain position just so a big 'impact' player can enter the fray late on when they can really make a difference. Players already out there are knackered and then a lump of muscle comes on, six foot four, 120 kilos, and starts slamming into them like they're made of matchsticks. Italy admitted they'd kept their best front row on the bench until the second half in a recent Six Nations game. South Africa did something similar when they came out victorious in the 2019 Rugby World Cup. With six forwards on the bench, they were able to introduce what became known as the 'Bomb Squad'. Great tactic – but one that will eventually shatter bodies and minds. Don't just take my word for it. Sir Clive Woodward, who played in the amateur era, has said that if he played now he'd get wiped out.

'The use of substitutes has sent the game the wrong way,' he says. 'Part of the game should be about fitness; about playing for eighty or a hundred minutes. Bring on fresh guys against guys who aren't so fresh and you've got a mismatch. That's dangerous. My big vision to win the World Cup wasn't based on power – to me it was more about aerobic fitness. If you become fit enough, you become powerful anyway.'

In 2021, some of the biggest names in the game, including my old mate Sir Ian McGeechan, wrote to World Rugby chairman Sir Bill Beaumont stating that the professional game had become 'unnecessarily dangerous'. In the letter they pointed out that with eight substitutes, it has effectively become twenty-three-a-side, with some players training accordingly, 'prioritising power over aerobic capacity . . . leading to more collisions and in the latter stages numerous fresh "giants" crashing into tiring opponents'. Those legends, who know a thing or two about the game, propose the number of substitutes be limited to four and used only in the case of injury. I couldn't agree more.

The letter also backs the view of former Wales and Lions skipper Sam Warburton that someone will die live on TV if action is not forthcoming. Let's just think about that – a man, an absolute hero of the game, who played seventy-four times for his country, predicting that unless the authorities act, someone will die in front of millions on TV.

Bill Ribbans, a consultant in trauma and orthopaedic surgery I know from my Northampton days, has described meeting one of the new breed of outsized professionals head-on as 'like being hit by a truck'. He believes that tackling such an opponent could put a force of a fifth of a tonne through a player's shoulder. This talk of bigger players isn't just make-believe. Analysis has revealed that top-level players in the eighties weighed on average 14 stone and stood at 5 feet 11 inches. In 2020, the average English Premiership player weighed 16 stone 3 pounds and was 6 feet 1 inch. Remember that's the average – there will be many packing considerably more power. World Rugby's own figures show the average number of tackles per game has almost tripled in the last three decades from ninety-four in 1987 to 257 in 2019. How many warnings need to be issued, statistics produced, ex-players and medical experts speak up before the sport starts to listen? If it was twenty years ago and you didn't understand what those big impacts did to people, then fair enough. It's professional sport and the goal is to win. But now that we do understand, the idea that it continues is wrong and sad. So many times, the response of the rugby authorities is 'We are conducting research.' How much research do these people need? The evidence is right in front of their eyes. Some of it is living and breathing – at present.

It's not just rugby. All of a sudden, it seems like every sporting body can't wait to explain what research they're doing. But some of these studies have been going for years and years. It was only because myself and others spoke out that their hands were forced.

It's been shocking to me how many people at the top level in sports administration are either clueless, arrogant, or a mixture of both. And that is why this sore has been allowed to fester so long. It's the easiest thing in the world to say, 'We're doing research,' but where actually are the results? Where's the action? You can't keep saying 'research, research, research' when people are losing their minds and dying. Neurological problems ranging from dementia to epilepsy and post-concussive syndrome – headaches, dizziness, issues with concentration and memory – aren't going to be banished by a surface approach. The fact is that under the current regulations in my sport there are players out there right now who will end up like me. To stop that happening, action has to be immediate. Rugby needs to stop protecting itself and start protecting those who play it.

Until that happens, its governing bodies will be accused of just paying lip service. They need to start backing up their words with substance. A responsible governing body assesses risk and makes the necessary changes. It doesn't sit back and spout 'research'. The information is out there now – deal with it. The instinct for self-protection has to go. What's happening to people is way too important for that.

Truth is the knowledge has been there for decades about the dangers of concussion. Bill Beaumont retired from the sport in 1982 because of it, and he wasn't even training full-time. Clive Woodward recalls times from his playing days in the eighties when players took blows with no concussion protocols in place.

'On one occasion,' he says, 'I got knocked out and literally walked to the side of the pitch, climbed across the barrier, and went and sat in the crowd. Les Cusworth [Clive's Leicester colleague] was wondering where the hell I was. The crowd in the stand were shouting, 'He's here, Les! Next to us!' I just jumped back over the barrier and went back on. There was no question of stopping me. Everyone was just laughing their heads off.'

Clive now describes his memory as 'hopeless'. 'Quite often my wife says to me, 'You've had a great life – you've just got to remember it!'

Clearly, there will have been people playing in the amateur era severely affected by concussion. But in all that time since, what has actually come along to battle head injury? I can think only of the scrum cap, which when you think about it is virtually pointless. When your head is impacted, scrum cap or not, it still causes violent movement in the skull; it still harms the brain. I tried wearing a scrum cap a couple of times but soon gave up. It made me too hot and also, because I have an egg-shaped head with – ahem – 'modelling high cheekbones' (as I like to tell people, I was good-looking before I played rugby) it was hard to find one to fit. Worse, in those days, opposition players would twist the chinstrap so it would go incredibly tight and stop you breathing. I also noticed that people with scrum caps tended to get cut more above the eyes because the cap pulls their skin so taut that it's easily split. Having suffered a serious neck injury, I was also aware of a scrum cap adding to the risk of it happening again by giving me a false sense of security.

'How many concussions have you had?' a doctor once asked me. I wasn't entirely sure what constituted a concussion. 'Is that when you completely lose consciousness?' I asked.

'No,' he replied, 'that's not how you measure it. I'm talking about impacts to the head. Ongoing head impacts are just as risky as a few major concussions.'

Impacts to the head? I thought. *Bloody hell, if that's the criteria then I was concussed every single game and training session.* I think back in particular to scrums against French sides. In a scrum, opposing packs are supposed to come together from a starting point a metre away from each other. French teams would start at that metre and then, seeking to impose themselves in any way they could, back up a few more. I'd see them retreat – *OK, right, here we go!* From their new position, they'd charge full pelt and smash into us. How much weight was behind that impact? All going through our heads and necks. Look at it now and you wonder how it was ever allowed.

The French weren't unique in taking the game's physicality to its extremes. Lots of teams would have 'enforcers' – players expected to tread on a player on the ground, to be getting the punches in. I'm not saying my era was the only one to experience tough rugby. When William Webb Ellis first picked up the ball and ran with it during a school football match in 1823, I expect it wasn't long before someone steamrollered him to the ground. But the sport the professional game morphed into by the 2000s was an ugly and bastardised version of that which came earlier.

The doctor's question made me realise that concussion has for too long been thought of as being laid out unconscious, like a boxer on the canvas, when actually it operates in degrees far more refined. Yes, there are those big impacts, but over the course of a career there are also thousands of sub-concussive injuries – the knocks, the jolts, the sudden twists – that a player takes in their stride as part of the game. The brain is shaken but without any obvious immediate result. Over the course of a ten- to fifteen-year career, because of the sheer number of rucks, tackles, carries, mauls and scrums that make up the average game, a player is likely to suffer tens of thousands of such blows. But that doesn't make it normal any more than it makes it right. A knock or a jolt to the head causes damage – it's as simple as that. Perhaps there would be better awareness of the seriousness of the issue if we dropped the word 'concussion' altogether and described an impact for what is – a traumatic brain injury. We could do the same with early-onset dementia – let's be up front and call it brain damage.

◈

I back the calls by Progressive Rugby, set up by former England international James Haskell, to establish ground rules for change in the sport. Progressive Rugby believes that World Rugby needs to accept that playing professional rugby can lead to CTE and other neurodegenerative diseases. It also wants limits on contact in training and the number of substitutes per game, as well as designated concussion spotters to have the authority to remove players showing visible symptoms, greater education on the issue of concussion, and better aftercare. I would add that rugby also needs more stringently to implement its existing laws. There are rules about dangerous tackling in both codes but they're utterly pointless if not put into practice.

I understand when people say I want to inflict on others a type of rugby I never had to play. I share that concern for the sport. Let's face it, who wants to turn up to a rugby match to see two teams slapping each other on the back for eighty minutes? But actually, if you look at the proposals for change, the essential nature of the match-day game remains the same. The improvements are about ensuring that players are not receiving endless and entirely pointless knocks in training, that contact laws are properly enforced, and that head trauma is scrutinised rigorously following a series of strict protocols. If rugby is to survive, these changes are non-negotiable. It's common sense. Sport changes over time, and the demands of professionalism, the raising of the stakes, the introduction of a business model, the desperation for both survival and success, change it more than anything. Professional rugby union began twenty-five years ago, but it might as well be a century for how much the game has moved on. The game at the top level has morphed into something way different from what people might have seen on *Rugby Special* on a Sunday afternoon in the seventies.

It is also entirely possible that there is plenty we have yet to learn about the brain and the effect of impact trauma. What we have seen so far may just be the foothills of a vast and ugly mountain. I look at Rob Burrow, the former Leeds Rhinos international, the bravest and most inspirational of men, so dreadfully struck down by motor neurone disease. At below 10 stone and just 5 feet 4 inches, across a sixteen-year career Rob was routinely tackling players twice his size. The link has yet definitively to be made between Rob's sporting life and the illness he has endured with such great humility, humour and courage, but it's hard not to wonder if one didn't lead to the other.

Those who run the game must address the facts about brain injury if thousands more are not to be left paying the highest possible price for playing rugby – to be left mere ghosts of their former selves. That's not scaremongering; that's fact. If nothing changes, what's to stop what happened to me and hundreds of others – the ones we know about – happening to those out there right now on the rugby field? To make people safe costs money, and that's why the game has to properly invest at all levels to make sure that happens.

No one wants to rock the boat, but it's gone way beyond that. It's obvious to me that, if others are to be saved from my fate, someone has to keep on shouting.

Chapter 17

PRIME WITNESS

I never wanted to be back in the public eye. In all honesty, my instinct is to shut the door on the world and get on with my life. Being in the newspapers, talked about on TV, and the centre of the hottest topic in every rugby club bar in the land was about as far away from the life I had in early 2020 as it could possibly be. My natural habitat was not in the media glare. It was on the canal with my fishing rod or messing about in the garden with the kids. That all changed as soon as it became clear that, to protect the long-term security of my family, I would be the highest-profile player in the test case led by Richard Boardman and sports concussion legal specialists Rylands Law against World Rugby, England Rugby and Wales Rugby Union.

It was obvious from the start that persuading the rugby authorities to open the purse strings and pay compensation for their alleged negligence in failing to protect me and others from concussive and sub-concussive injuries was going to be challenging. However, Richard and his fellow lawyers, representing me and an ever-increasing number of ex-players, all part of the first generation to have played an entire career of full-time professional rugby, were always optimistic of the right result, a belief based on a solid legal base. Any sporting body owes a duty of care to those who play the game, and yet in rugby, contact in training was never restricted and adequate concussion protocols had, if anything, become more lax.

The mountain of legal jargon left me cold, but I could see we had a strong case. Rugby had failed to act on clear evidence of the risks of head injury, just as it had failed to reflect on the impact of the new revved-up power game that emerged when the sport went professional. I was the living, breathing evidence of their culpability. Steve Thompson – exhibit number one. I was joined on the public stage by, among others, ex-England flanker Michael Lipman, who was once carried off the pitch five times in one season. Michael's symptoms are horribly familiar – mood swings, disorientation and forgetfulness have become part of his daily life. On one occasion he left his baby unattended for ninety minutes. Then there was former Leicester, Gloucester and Rotherham flanker Neil Spence, afflicted by speech problems, anxiety attacks and depression. Neil used to judge how well he'd performed by how fuzzy-headed he felt at the final whistle. As a coach he once drove straight past the nursery where he was due to pick up his children and instead parked up at another school and started setting up a training session. All Blacks legend, former tighthead prop Carl Hayman, joined the action against World Rugby after being diagnosed with early onset dementia aged just forty-one. He'd been suffering from headaches, memory loss and had contemplated taking his own life. He was stunned when he couldn't remember his son's middle name when applying for a passport. Then of course there was Alix Popham, whose troubles had made me realise I might have my own difficulties.

And yet, as the court case wound on, I found myself going from feeling really positive – I knew we were in the right, and what we were doing was exactly what we should be doing – to suddenly thinking the whole thing was a colossal waste of time. *People like us always get fucked over. We never win. We're always put back in our box and told to shut up.* I watched the film *Dark Waters*, which tells the true story of the residents of a New Jersey town suffering serious health issues believed to be the result of drinking water polluted by chemicals from a nearby factory, and the lawyer desperately trying to get the company responsible to pay compensation. Those poor people wait years and years while the claims go through endless legal processes, to-ing and fro-ing between insurance companies. I'm not sure I can handle that kind of timescale – the pressure, the not knowing, the endless nagging at the back of my mind. It's so hard on Steph too, at a time when we've got so much going on in our lives, when we are trying to work out what tomorrow might look like, to constantly have that uncertainty. How can we plan for my care, for the family's future, when we have no idea what our financial situation will be? Some people might say, 'Let's get out there while we can and blow whatever we've got,' but I'm not like that. I want to plan so I can make sure that Steph and the kids are OK. I've had my life. I'm not bothered about being pampered in big hotels, splashing cash in car showrooms. All that matters now is looking after the kids and looking after Steph; making sure they can live without constant money worries. As it is, there's nothing set aside to look after us. I've got a family. I look at the price of care and it frightens me. It cannot be left to them to shoulder that burden.

In the same way some people think I am being ungrateful to rugby, biting the hand that fed me, others accuse me of being greedy – *He earned good money for running around with a ball and now he wants more?* If people think I'm being greedy then perhaps they could tell me what exactly the going rate is for losing your mind. They might also want to consider how much it costs to care for someone with dementia. And how big the loss is of their earning potential. People have an idea that because it's professional sport everyone's a multi-millionaire on fifty grand a week. Don't get me wrong, we were on good money, but nowhere near enough to set us up for life. And how much money is enough to justify dementia? It doesn't matter how much money a person earns, in any area of life no one deserves that.

What they do deserve is the organisation that has some responsibility for their demise to have the common decency to put its hand up and admit it. Do that and you give those who have suffered something much more valuable than financial settlement – you give them mental settlement. Considering how many players are going through the turmoil of concussion-related illnesses, the importance of freeing them from the legal quicksand and allowing them to carry a lighter load couldn't be more important. Like everyone else, I want to move on from legal talk, from witness statements, from trying to take in endless reports. The court case is the one thing I do want to forget, and I can't. It's no good saying to me that the wheels of justice move slowly. It means nothing and can never be a justification for the stress that so many people, not least the players' families, have been put through.

Truth is, all this should have been sorted out long ago. Evidence of the consequences of head trauma have been swirling around rugby for almost fifty years. It's no good hiding behind CTE only being diagnosed by a post-mortem dissection of the brain. The Concussion Legacy Foundation is a non-profit organisation which, alongside the Boston Brain Bank, revealed the presence of CTE in 110 out of 111 former NFL players whose brains it examined. Contact sport can no longer fall back on the post-mortem get-out clause. It's an argument that doesn't work in America any more and neither should it here. That ship has sailed. How many criteria do there have to be to prove a point? It has to be accepted that brain trauma causes CTE and that's the end of it.

The Concussion Legacy Foundation, based on both sides of the Atlantic, is now turning its attention to rugby where, as first-generation professionals such as myself reach middle age, it expects to find a similarly devastating story. I have met the foundation's chief executive, Chris Nowinski. It was Chris who persuaded the family of renowned NFL defensive back Andre Waters for permission to send a sample of brain tissue to Bennet Omalu, whom I mentioned earlier, after Andre killed himself with a shotgun. Examination revealed the tissue to be similar to that of an eighty-five-year-old. Waters was forty-four when he took his own life. He had developed CTE. 'I stopped counting my concussions at fifteen,' Waters once said. 'I wouldn't say anything, I'd just sniff smelling salts and go back out there.'

Chris, a neuroscientist and former Harvard American football player, has first-hand experience of brain injury. He suffered serious post-concussion symptoms after a kick in the head during his second career as a WWE wrestler. The issue alerted him to concussion's potential for long-term harm and the lack of knowledge and concern displayed by many sports.

'Let's stop the bleeding,' is his rallying cry. 'Let's not ruin anyone else's life because we think people need to practise getting hit in the head every day to become good rugby players.'

His is another significant and highly knowledgeable voice calling for immediate action to limit full-contact training and address the endless brain and body-shattering nature of the game. With the brains of American football players forming the vast majority of those studied by his foundation, Chris sees it as vital to build a rugby evidence base. As obvious it is that there's a problem, beyond any reasonable doubt – rugby players are coming forward with more clinical symptoms than even some NFL players – the experts will still need to prove the situation. And so I have made a major decision. When I die, my brain will be donated to the Concussion Legacy Project, formed by the Concussion Legacy Foundation UK and the Jeff Astle Foundation, to aid scientific research on CTE. Change needs numbers, and if change is what comes about then I'm happy for one of those numbers to be me.

Brain donation is very personal and emotional, and not something anyone would imagine themselves thinking about at such a young age, but while there's a chance it could help others not to end up in the same state as me, it's something I'm determined to do. Steph's fine – well, as fine as any partner can be – with me going down that route, which is a very big thing in itself. I can't imagine it's nice for her having to think about something so bound up with death. The taking away of the brain – the very core of a loved one – is so poignant and final. It means I won't be buried or cremated whole, something which can be very important, comforting even, for those left behind. It's a big decision and there has to be understanding and compassion for those families who can't bear to let such an essential part of a person – their personality, their character, their love, all tied up in the brain – go. It's horrendous that playing a sport should mean a family is ever put in a position of having to choose.

Obviously, while everyone concerned – not least myself – hopes it will be a while before my brain ends up under the knife, the fact I'm making the pledge shows my absolute belief in the work of the foundation and its ability to force change. That's why I'm heartened to see I'm not the only rugby player to have pledged to donate my brain to science. Former All Blacks James Broadhurst and Ben Afeaki, and ex-Wallaby prop Toby Smith, all of whom left the game because of head injuries, are doing the same, as is Aussie rugby league giant Peter Sterling. The family of Dave Bolton, the Wigan legend who died aged eighty-three following a long battle with dementia, also made the incredible gesture of donating his brain to science after his death.

While reassured by the determination of rugby players to highlight brain trauma and CTE, I can't help but wonder how many more examples, how many more families put through the emotional upset of brain donation, there have to be. CTE barely occurs in the general population but is endemic in contact sport. Forget just rugby and the NFL, Aussie Rules footballers Danny Frawley, who died in a car crash, and Shane Tuck, who took his own life, were found to have CTE. In baseball, where collisions, such as between catchers and runners, are more common than you might think, Ryan Freel, who also killed himself, became the first Major League Baseball player to be diagnosed with CTE, while Canadian ice hockey winger Derek Boogaard, who died of an accidental drug and alcohol overdose, was found to have suffered from advanced CTE at the age of just twenty-eight. Closer to home, five members of England's World Cup-winning football team have developed dementia. Jack Charlton, Nobby Stiles, Ray Wilson and

Martin Peters all died of the illness. Sir Bobby Charlton is still suffering from the condition. Five out of eleven can hardly be described as a coincidence. I'll be honest, it makes me feel sick when I hear about how pros would practise headers back then – a ball hung from the ceiling smashing against the skull again and again. That's before regular heading practice on the training pitch.

Of course, it's not just men. Many women play contact sports and there's plenty of evidence to suggest they are being affected, too. Aussie Rules star and American football quarterback Jacinda Barclay took her own life aged just twenty-nine after a spell of mental illness. Faced with her damaged brain, experts at the Australian Sports Brain Bank described it as a ticking time bomb. Brandi Chastain, meanwhile, one of the biggest names in women's football, scoring the winning penalty for the USA in the 1999 World Cup final, has also agreed to donate her brain to the Concussion Legacy Foundation after fearing her memory issues might be due to her years heading a ball.

I could fill the rest of this book and a dozen more with the names and stories of others whose brains have been addled by CTE. How much more evidence does there need to be about the link between contact sport and brain damage? It couldn't be more obvious. The research we really need is not whether CTE exists – cognitive tests and brain scans can provide evidence of CTE before death – it's how to treat it. We need people to confront sports and ask why they're not making reforms, because for any sport to say change isn't needed is basically to argue that CTE is part of impact sport and we're comfortable giving it to children.

Rather than post-mortem, better surely to create a system which allows ongoing and compulsory examination of a player's brain while they're alive? A 'player's MOT' would involve the same DTI scan that revealed the damage suffered by me. The upshot is a much improved chance of identifying CTE. If a player has a DTI scan at the very beginning of their professional career, there is then a baseline from which any deterioration can be measured. That might mean players having to retire before they've barely got started. Yes, that's sad. But it's better than ending up like me. Rugby is a game. There are plenty of other games.

Neurosurgeons have long been telling the game that permanent damage can come off the back of even a single concussion. I'm not quite sure why no one listened. Perhaps they found the data a bit dry. Just numbers. But numbers equate to lives; to brains crashing around in skulls. Year in, year out, players are being let down, and the consequences are terrible. Now, because the truth about dementia is both undeniable and has been made very public, no governing body of any contact sport can sit back and pretend nothing is wrong.

Rugby has made some forward progress. If officials deem it necessary, players must undergo a pitchside head injury assessment. Targeting an opponent's head has also been made an immediate red card. But really, until the game implements a concerted and wide-ranging set of measures, it is doing nothing more than sticking an occasional plaster on a permanent gaping wound. There needs to be surgery, the like of which happened in American football after Bennet Omalu's determination revealed the connection between the game and CTE, resulting ultimately in a group of former players starting a class action against the NFL, which delivered meaningful change and a billion-dollar settlement. Not that it came easy. There was a concerted campaign of doubt towards the research. Team owners believed the bullshit, and the doctors talking to them were often in their pay. Eventually, however, the game's ruling body reduced the amount of training impacts and allowed just one contact training session a week. I look at those restrictions and totally see it as something that rugby can embrace. It is estimated that such simple changes will reduce the number of career impacts for NFL players by 70,000. The ruination of American football the doom-mongers predicted never happened. It remains as popular as ever.

I'm envious of those ex-NFL players in as much as they have resolution. There have been times when I've thought that will never come. It's been hard to keep having to go over and over my dementia experience as each stage of the legal fight has progressed. It's something which all too easily flicks a negative switch in my brain and makes me prone to downward mood swings – *If they win the case, where does that leave me? What do I do then?* I start taking things personally and feel animosity towards the sport's governing bodies for the position I'm in; for what can very easily be taken, in the black and white world of the legal process, as their lack of concern and compassion for my condition. I know as well that feeling like that helps no one. It eats you up and makes you bitter. I don't want to be like that. I can't waste whatever time I've got left on bitterness. I have to be positive. I have to win my case to show that what they've done is wrong. I want sport – all sport – to take the matter seriously and deliver the appropriate steps.

So much of the state we're in now is down to sport being allowed to mark its own homework for way too long. People have been brainwashed to think that because sport isn't a normal workplace, you can't have the same expectations; that sport is so dangerous it would be impossible to regulate like anywhere else. After all, in most sports there's a one hundred per cent injury rate. At some point, anyone who plays sport will be injured. That's what those who oppose change hide behind – 'It's not a normal environment.' Fine, but that doesn't mean anything goes. You can't just say, 'Sport's a special case; we can't change it.' Not now the knowledge of the problem is there. That's not right any more than it's fair on the players. Again, it also needs to be remembered that a lot of those players are children.

In every other area of life, the government lays down the relevant health and safety legislation. The idea that because it's sport these life and death matters can be left to governing bodies is ridiculous. In my other life, working in holes in the ground, a long-term physical difficulty resulting from that job would be classed as an industrial injury. There are strict boundaries within which the construction industry operates, otherwise they would be in breach of their duty of care. It's as if sport doesn't matter; that because there is always a risk of injury it should exist out of the normal criteria for health and safety. While other industries are forced to act, sport just drags its feet. Rugby has been snail-like in its reaction, as has football. It's two decades since a coroner ruled that Jeff Astle's dementia was entirely consistent with heading a ball. Research shows that ex-footballers are more than three times more likely to die of dementia than others in the same age range. As Dawn Astle says, 'Football has failed to act and failed to protect its players – men, women, children, all at risk, potentially, with no restrictions, unprotected, uninformed. If the sport is left to its own devices as it is, it will just do what it wants to do.' The game has restricted heading in age-group training but may yet need to go further if it is to convince the players of the future, and their parents or carers, that the dementia risk has been reduced to acceptable levels.

There was once a point where every time I heard the words 'health and safety' I'd be on my high horse saying the world has gone to pot. But that was because I was ignorant of the reality. Now I've looked around and properly taken in the risks, I can see that there's nothing wrong with keeping people safe if you can. I don't believe in wrapping the world in cotton wool, but if there are obvious areas of concern, why on earth wouldn't you do something about them?

It's so simple, even someone with a brain injury – like me – could get the ball rolling. Why not boil it down to seven rules we could start to implement right now, tomorrow, and begin improving player safety? Call it what you want, but for what it's worth, here is my own seven-point manifesto for change:

1. Honesty

Call concussion what it really is – a traumatic brain injury. Speak about it in those terms and immediately the situation changes. Whatever walk of life, if people are suffering traumatic brain injuries, then those around them have to take the situation seriously and act.

2. Impact Reduction

If we're going to reduce head trauma, then there's a blindingly obvious way of doing so – reduce the number of collisions. Impacts in a match environment are one thing; to routinely build them into training sessions is entirely another. It's a game of skill (supposedly), not a demolition derby. Limit contact in training and you limit the scope for damage. Even with my own irreparably damaged brain I can work that one out. Why can't those who run rugby do the same?

3. Player Passports

We might occasionally google symptoms when we have a sore throat. But when the search engine throws up tonsilitis as a possible cause, we don't then grab a knife, clear the kitchen table and operate on ourselves.

In everyday life, we place our long-term health in the hands of experts. Why aren't we doing the same with rugby? Player passports – an annual MOT – deliver constantly updated data from which any physical or mental decline can be measured and acted on.

4. Concussion Management

Build this into the game at all levels – NOW. No longer can we have children staggering around pitches, allowed to carry on because of an 'it'll be all right' attitude to protection, encouraged by the 'toughening up' nonsense spewed by some in the game. Concussion protocols have to be strictly implemented. Those who fail to do so should be removed from the game.

5. Concussion Holidays

A player suffering a suspected concussion should not be allowed back on the field for a minimum of three weeks. It doesn't matter who they are – a kid playing for their school or the number one star in the world. We forget sometimes what rugby is: a sport. If someone misses three weeks it's not the end of their world – but it could be if they don't.

6. Substitutions

With eyes closed, or possibly open for those who believe major collision equals good TV (this is real life not a YouTube video), a situation has arisen whereby teams can throw on eight fresh substitutes and use them to smash a vulnerable and wearied opposition. The potential consequences of this are obvious – well, they should be. Substitutes should only ever be used in the case of injuries.

7. Pitchside Personnel

Jockeys often make the point that horse racing is the only sport where the participants are pursued by an ambulance. I'm not suggesting a new position – blindside paramedic – but it's vital that those with a level of medical know-how, on top of basic first aid, are present at rugby matches of all levels. There has to be proper, guaranteed protection.

Thankfully, the situation over concussion in sport has now at least been recognised. In 2021, The Department for Digital, Culture, Media and Sport released a report, *Concussion in Sport*, recommending that all sports should use a UK-wide standard definition for concussion, while the Health and Safety Executive should establish a national framework for the reporting of brain injuries in sport. It is also pushing for UK Sport, which oversees elite sport, to pay for a medical officer, with the power to prevent athletes from competing, at every major sporting event. If recommendations such as these go unhindered, then the numbers left with serious brain trauma from sport will reach epidemic proportions. Already, Richard Boardman has said he believes up to 50 per cent of former professional rugby players could end up with neurological complications in retirement. We're not talking one or two unlucky people here. We're talking thousands. Luck isn't part of the equation. The way rugby is now, lasting issues from head trauma are almost unavoidable. I hear about the sport's plans for a brain health clinic for retired players aged thirty to fifty-five. Great, except the damage is happening to players in their twenties. No point acting after the horse has bolted. Those players need protecting. That's partly the job of the Rugby Players' Association (RPA), the representative body of players in England. But if even a fraction of their funding comes from the RFU, how can they ever claim to be impartial? It can never be the case that a players' organisation is compromised. You, the RPA, are there to protect the players. If that's your job, then do it. Don't leave it up to those at the sharp end of the fight.

◈

If the determination of myself and others to fight the rugby authorities through the courts means that, ultimately, they will make root and branch reforms to the game, then the hard work will have been worth it, because those changes will save a lot of pain and, I believe, more than a few lives. But I really do wish I didn't have to do it. My life right now would be a lot simpler and far less strained without any of it. It's stress heaped upon stress. I just want the case completed. I don't want it constantly hovering over me. Sometimes I find myself sitting on the side of the bed panicking and rocking.

Other times I'll message my solicitor, looking for reassurance, evidence that I'm doing the right thing. But there can never be total reassurance because so much of what I'm dealing with is unknown.

What keeps me going is the absolute and unshakeable belief that the way I and so many others have been treated is wrong; that I might be able to make my family's life secure and live my final conscious years without the stress of wondering if they'll be OK when the illness does its worst. I live my life to give my children better opportunities than I had. I didn't have much, but on the other hand I never had a parent who was dependent on me for care. I want my kids to know that if they're away living their own lives, they can do so without worry because I'm being professionally looked after. I don't want them not to go to university, or miss out on a job, or whatever, because of worrying about their mum having to lift me into the bath, or me wandering off. They're amazing kids and I know if they see their mum struggling they will never reach their own potential. I want them to know all that is taken care of. I want them to be able to fly, free of the burden of me. A dad doesn't get looked after by his family. A dad looks after them. To have that potentially turned on its head makes me feel terrible. Overwhelming guilt that I have let them down accompanies me everywhere. But that's not the worst of it. The thought of me being trapped in the wreckage of my own mind somehow aware of my children feeding, washing, dressing me, makes me feel sick. If that ever does happen, I hope I am far gone. I mean really far gone. I can't ever be aware of it. I can't ever be tortured in that way.

Of all the things that this court case has been said to be about, the one word that never appears is 'dignity'. I'm a person who, by necessity a lot of the time, has always stood on his own two feet. I've prided myself on being independent. Now that's slipping from my control – and I'm not alone. All across the rugby landscape, former players are seeing their ability to look after themselves stripped away. At their lowest points, their heads are full of the same dark thoughts as mine – spoon-feeding, sponge baths, someone wiping my backside like I'm a child, tucking me into bed. This can never be a court case with winners. How can anyone win when so much will be lost? What it can be about, appropriately enough – and I'll allow myself the smallest of ironic smiles when I write this – is peace of mind. We need to know our future care will preserve our dignity, and those of our loved ones, for as long as humanly possible. How can anyone who has lost their ability to steer their own life be denied that?

Chapter 18

VANISHING POINT

A s I've mentioned, when I started to talk about the collisions that caused my dementia and the fact I was seeking a settlement, there were more than a few people whose first thought wasn't, *Bloody hell, that's terrible, a bloke in his forties who can't remember his wife's name.* Instead, they went straight to, *Well, I didn't hear him complaining about it at the time.*

At first I felt angry when I heard that kind of comment, but then, actually, when I thought about it, I realised those people were making the point for me. How on earth could I complain about any of it? I didn't know it was happening.

Play rugby for any length of time and it's a given you're going to end up with physical issues. In my case I broke my neck twice. My shoulders, elbows and knees are blown to pieces. I accept that. No problem. All part of the job I chose. But I never knew what was happening to my brain.

How could I? If I had known I'd have stopped in my mid-twenties, just like a lot of players are now. Yes, at first that would have been a kick in the nuts, but I'd have my life now.

The reason I'm 'complaining', as some people put it, is that the knowledge already existed that the mangling we saw happen to our bodies was also happening to the inside of our heads. And that knowledge was ignored. My only concern after a knock to the head was how quickly I could get back on my feet again. The number of brain cells that had just been irreparably damaged was not part of my internal conversation. Why would it be? I was a player not a medic. There are people in rugby whose job it is to ensure the protection of players. I wasn't one of them. I wouldn't have been able to do their job any more than they'd have been able to do mine. It's for the same reason I don't MOT my own car. I haven't got a clue what goes on under the bonnet and so I leave it to a mechanic. And I'd expect that mechanic to shout up if they thought there might be a problem that could send the vehicle heading straight into a ditch.

In rugby, there were clearly people with knowledge about head injuries and yet nothing was done. People say you should know your own body. Fine. I know if I'm hurting. I know if I've strained a side or twisted an ankle. But the inside of my skull? I'm sorry, I haven't a clue. I don't see the bruises, don't see the blood. That lack of signposting continues to be a huge problem. Think about it. If you're in your twenties, in the prime of your life, playing for a professional club, possibly your country, earning good money, are you going to listen to all the sad stories of those who lost their minds? Are you going to want to walk off the pitch after a collision and potentially lose your place to the next cab on the rank? At that point you're living the life you dreamed of, a life for which you've bust a gut since you were a kid. Wild horses wouldn't drag you away from it. That's why players are the last people who should be allowed any part in decision-making on head injury.

I know for sure that if I could hitch a ride in the Tardis and return to my teenage years, I'd much rather not have laid eyes on a rugby ball. Of course, I don't for one second include Steph and the kids in that. They're in my life – they are my life – precisely because of my career in rugby and are the best things to have ever happened to me. What I mean is I could have had a normal life and still been in a good place mentally instead of the mess I find myself in now.

I hear retired players who say they'd do it all over again. They must be mad. Either that or somehow have absolutely no one around them who would be affected. If they say those words in the full knowledge that loved ones could be dragged into their mental turmoil then they're offering a very selfish point of view. OK, so right now, dementia couldn't be further removed from your mind. One day it might be closer than you could ever imagine. It will parcel up and dispatch any memory of those good times. At which point you might very well think the same as me: *If I can't remember any of it, why the hell did I bother?*

Perhaps they have yet to face the possibility of how life might look in a few years' time. Perhaps they can't bring themselves to think about it. I can't erect that barrier. For me, it's demolished. Gone. I see my kids who, the same as anyone else, I want to make happy, put a roof over their heads and provide for. But how long am I going to be capable of doing any work? Already, I'm limited to strictly physical duties. My ability to deal with planning and paperwork has gone. OK, had I been diagnosed while playing, my rugby career would have finished earlier. I'd have been disappointed. But I'd have got on with life and by now would be well set in an established job with a secure long-term income. Instead, I'm having to rediscover myself at forty-three with brain damage.

Consciously and subconsciously I'm adapting to the new me. I know there are people who must look at me working on the tools and wonder what the hell has happened to me – *Hang on, didn't he win the World Cup? What's he doing messing about down holes? Poor bastard must be right down on his luck.* But I don't want to work in a high-pressure environment. I know for sure I couldn't manage it nowadays anyway. I find peace in doing a normal job. I started out working on building sites and chances are if rugby hadn't come along that's where I'd have ended up – and I'd have been perfectly happy with that. Money has never been a big thing for me.

The issue now is that even that source of income – a normal physical hands-on job – is under threat. Even with manual work my focus can be affected. One minute I'll think of a solution to a problem and the next it's gone. Same if I have a Zoom call about a job. People say I come over really well, but that's because if I have an important meeting I'll prep for it the day before. Truth is, I'll come off that call and not have a Scooby what's been said. The upshot is I can find myself blagging a bit – which in itself feels terrible because it's something I've never done. I'll bullshit my way through things. Afterwards Steph will be laughing. 'What went on there then?' And I'll say to her, 'I haven't got a clue.' I repeat things other people say to make it sound like I'm keyed in to what's going on.

Physical repetitive work I'm OK with, but I know the time will come when insurance companies will look at me uncertainly in terms of working in that environment. Where will that leave me financially? Which is another unseen element of dementia – it wrecks people's earning potential. Just at the time when people are desperate to give themselves and those around them some security, the world of work slams its doors on them. Many ex-sportspeople, for example, earn a few quid by looking back on their careers at rugby club dos. I used to do the same. But how can I do that now when I can barely remember any of it? The same goes for media work. In previous years, for instance, I've done interviews to coincide with Lions tours. No chance of that now. If I can't make comparisons with my own experiences, what's the point?

I also used to work at Twickenham in an ambassadorial role for England's home games. After suing the RFU I'm fairly sure I won't be asked back. In essence, financially, over the past five years, my life has fallen apart. My kids aren't spoiled but I want to give them a good life. Now I wonder how. What happens when they're a bit older and they need driving lessons? Sounds a daft question, but little things like that flit in and out of my mind. When it comes to money and the future it's such an intricate web I have to negotiate. If I had to work three jobs and weekends to make my family happy, I'd do it. But I can't any more. I've gone from a plan to carry on working forever to having no idea what or where I'll be in a matter of a few years. I feel like in no time I've gone from being able to do loads of stuff to having just a tiny shrunken pot of options. I'm in a massive panic all the time. I can't just stop working. I need to do something.

Easy to forget also how the sudden absence of work adds to dementia sufferers' social isolation. More and more they're cut off from something that would have been a major source of mental stimulation and company. Working out and about flushing out water mains has given me something that makes me happy. I always wanted to work outside, something physical which I can just get on and do with a gang of mates. That's my comfort zone, what makes me happy, same as being with a bunch of mates on a rugby team made me happy back in the day. After a few days working with Shaun, he turned to me. 'You're one of the biggest disappointments of my life,' he told me. 'Because you're so stupid and normal.' Stupid and normal – for me, that was the best compliment anyone could ever pay me. I just like to get on with a job and enjoy it along the way. Steph says that in all the years she's known me she's never seen me happier in work than I am now. Even in Dubai when I was involved in big deals it wasn't truly making me happy. I was doing it because I felt I should. A job like this I'm doing because I love it. I'm always at my best when I'm surrounded by a group of people I like and trust. I'm just a normal bloke who stepped into an abnormal world and stepped back again. But now I face losing that as well. I always thought I was going to be one of those blokes you see on the sites – in his sixties but still going, loving it. My attitude has always been why retire? People say when you're retired every day's a holiday. But if every day's the same, a holiday is the one thing it really isn't. The thought of doing nothing leaves me cold. I believe we all have something to offer society. I never want to be someone who takes and never gives back, to sit on my arse and let everyone else do the hard graft. On the sites, everyone laughs because I like sweeping. For me, seeing somewhere neat and clean makes me feel good. It puts me in a good place. I see volunteers out litter-picking and hear people say, 'Why bother? What's the point?' But I totally get it. They're doing good and putting themselves in a good spot mentally as well. You might look at what I do as just flushing out pipes. But I really like it, especially compared to sitting in meetings trying to take in endless bits of useless information. I'll always try to work – even if I have to be put on a bungee rope so I don't wander off.

Not much chance of me disappearing from the brewery I part own – well, they do say 'Do what you love'! The Powder Monkey Brewing Co. is based in Gosport inside a historic gunpowder magazine near the naval base. 'Powder monkey' is what they used to call a kid who scurried around moving the gunpowder from a warship's hold to the cannons on deck. I even have a range of beers named after me. I've tested plenty of Hop & Hooker. Appropriately enough, Old Northamptonians Rugby Club was the first place to sell it.

There's something else I really do love that's come out of my involvement with Powder Monkey. Jim, the dad of my fellow director Mike McGeever, lives just down the road from me, and Mike, who's based down south, asked if I'd look in on him. The first time I went round to Jim's flat he was eating his Weetabix with a tie on, and the place was spotless. Jim might have had a stroke but he's always immaculate.

I soon found that, while essentially I was meant to be helping Jim out with his shopping, our trips to Tesco were actually doing a massive amount to help me, a remedy for what I'm going through. I meet Jim and I feel useful, like I'm doing something. When we come out we sit on a bench outside the shop, sometimes for an hour or more. We might not say much but I hear him breathing next to me. Sounds weird, I know, but it's the nicest sound. I turn round and see him taking in the fresh air, listening to the birds, with the sun on his face, and I know he's simply appreciating being alive. It's a leveller being with Jim. It makes me feel more appreciative of what I've got rather than thinking about what I'm going to lose.

Jim's just about the first properly old person I've ever got to know. I look at us wandering round the supermarket and think, *This must be Britain's most confused shopping trip!* The two of us blundering round that shop. 'Have you got the shopping bags?' 'No, I thought you'd got them.' But Jim can be sharp. He knows all the deals in Tesco. I'll put him a couple of microwave meals in the basket. 'No, no – get another and then you get the discount.'

He also won't be patronised. By all accounts, Jim was quite a tough character back in his day. One time we were out, Steph messaged me to say she had some friends coming round and to grab a couple of bottles of Prosecco.

'Put them in the trolley,' he said. 'I'll get those for you.'

'No, no, Jim. I wouldn't hear of it.'

We went back and forth like this a few times until eventually he snapped. 'For God's sake, Steve! Just let me get these for you!'

I smiled. 'Whoa! There he is! I knew he was in there some-where.' We both started laughing. 'You're definitely getting back to how you used to be, you miserable old bastard!'

The Prosecco incident was a lesson learned. It's important we still respect people whatever their age and condition and let them make decisions for as long as they can.

Going to see Jim has been an eye-opener. Every time I leave him I feel like crying. Whether that's because of what's happening to me, that I see a bit of future me in there, I'm not sure, but there is something very emotional about it.

My hope is I can find a satisfying and worthwhile future by finding a work project that not just encompasses my illness but makes it a central feature, helping and advising others so they have as much chance as humanly possible to stave off the tide of dementia. Sadly, this isn't a presence that can be nipped in the bud – you can't take a course of tablets and make it go away – but you can help yourself by getting fitter and making other lifestyle changes. I want to make people more aware of those elements. I might not be able to get up in front of an audience and talk about my rugby career any more, but I can talk about what's happened to me from a medical point of view and, hopefully, help others understand. I don't want people tiptoeing around me. If someone has a question, I'd rather they just came out and said it. For my part, I won't sit on the fence. I'll just come out and answer it. I want dementia to be talked about openly and not seen as something to be mentioned in whispers, as if it's somehow taboo. Look at the strides that have been made educating men about testicular cancer. I know players who began routinely checking themselves in the showers on the back of all those adverts on TV and in newspapers. Because of that they were diagnosed in time. Beforehand, no way would they have been checking themselves, be it in the showers or anywhere else. I actually went to see a doctor myself after finding a lump. Luckily it turned out to be nothing more than a cyst, but the point is I'd been spurred into action by the campaigning of others. That's the kind of awareness I want people of all ages to have about dementia, so when they start getting forgetful, or a relative becomes unpredictable or irrational, they can throw the illness straight into the mix as a possible cause.

More than that, I want to raise the profile of an illness that so often seems to be pushed to the back of the cupboard – better off out of view, unseen. I know how that feels. In an ideal world, a clinical plan involving a small case-management team would be drawn up for someone like me. Of course, we don't live in an ideal world and so that case-management team doesn't exist. I have a profile from rugby and so people have come forward to help me, but of course very few other patients have that good fortune.

◈

According to government statistics, in 2019 there were 66,424 deaths due to dementia and Alzheimer's disease. That amounts to 12.5 per cent of all deaths. Imagine if one in eight of us died on the roads? The outcry would be massive. With dementia, all we hear is silence. There are people now really trying to push dementia to the top of the health agenda, and I want to be one of them. Can we get those numbers down? Can we demand better treatment and help for families? Of course we can. It's not acceptable to hide the problem away like a dirty secret. These are people's lives. They deserve to be treated with dignity.

I know also, from what I have learned in the short time I've been diagnosed, that dementia affects a much broader spectrum than just the very old. There are a lot of much younger people suffering. We need to break the stereotype and allow those other people to come into view if we are to truly understand and address the dementia crisis unfolding in front of us.

I had originally meant to title this chapter 'The Future'. Truth is, there are millions of people in this country who have exactly zero idea what their future holds, either because they've been diagnosed with dementia or because a loved one is being slowly consumed by the illness, and myself and my family are no different. Is my dementia going to get worse quickly or might it level off for a few years? Look at what's happened with footballers. Some have gone downhill quickly while for others the decline has been much more prolonged.

Already I feel confused as to how quickly I'm deteriorating. Quite clearly, I'm forgetting stuff. I can't get away from the fact that I can look at a basic object and have no idea what the name for it is. That's in my face. But other times I meet people and they say that if they hadn't known beforehand they would never have suspected there was an issue. Although they might if they'd been in the passenger seat when I got lost at a roundabout. It happens. I was driving back from work the other week, at a roundabout I've been around a hundred times, and suddenly, out of nowhere, I had no idea where I was. I carried on and eventually saw something that gave me a reminder – 'Oh, I know where I am!'

All, really, I or anyone in my position can do is live day-to-day. Within that, I know I am slowly diminishing in a way that will increasingly pass me by. It's like watching your children grow up. Day by day they look the same but stand them by the door frame and make that pencil mark and it's three inches higher than the last. Growing, always growing. It feels sometimes like I'm heading the other way – vanishing, always vanishing.

I expect one day we'll meet halfway.

Chapter 19

FAMILY

My time's gone now. My time's about looking after the family – and them, in their own way, looking after me.

Saskia saw me staring at the dog again today. She knew straight away that, as ever, I was trying – and failing – to remember its name. 'It's Stan,' she said, and that was it, she was off on her way.

Same thing happens if I can't think of a word – she's straight in there making suggestions, helping me dredge it up – something I need more and more. Take yesterday – Steph asked me if I wanted a drink. 'Yes, coffee please,' I answered, 'and can I have it in a . . . er . . . erm . . .' I was floundering badly. 'One of these,' I said, holding up a mug. M-U-G. Three letters. Gone. So Saxon, Saskia, Slone and Seren, thanks – I'll take all the help I can get.

I'm forever proud of the children and how they are around me. They've adapted incredibly well to the situation, if anything wanting to be with me even more – even if having the help of a small army of under-tens is a stark and noisy reminder that the situation exists in the first place. I feel sad for them filling in the gaps in their dad's sentences or second-guessing what's bothering me – 'Dad, if it's your jacket you're looking for, it's in the car' – but at least now, as a family, to varying degrees we all understand. Before my diagnosis, my forgetfulness would cause friction. Steph and I bickered. Crossed wires all the time. Quite justifiably, she'd ask me why I'd not done something I'd told her I would, some bit of DIY perhaps. For my part I'd be aggrieved she hadn't done something she'd said she would, only for her to tell me, 'What are you on about? I told you I'd changed my mind. Why don't you ever take any notice?'

The kids were the same – 'Dad, you're silly you are. You promised you were going to do something and you haven't done it.' Sounds daft I know, but at times, bearing in mind I genuinely didn't know I'd promised something and not gone through with it, it felt like my entire family was ganging up on me. Now we all know there's a problem we can look at things in a different light. Some of the things I do (or don't do) – getting in the wrong door of the car, putting ice cream in the fridge – are so crazy that in the end all we can do is laugh about them.

For the kids, my little moments of insanity offer an opportunity to turn the tables. Whenever they do something a bit silly, I'll say to them, 'Dime Bar!' like the old Harry Enfield advert in which he plays a none-too-clever shopper tipping boxes of the things into his trolley. Now, when I start stumbling over words, stuttering a little, Seren has started doing it back to me – 'Daddy! Dime Bar!' Maybe one day she'll take it a step further and use Harry's catchphrase from that advert – 'That bloke's a nutter!' Hopefully, I'll still be able to comprehend enough to know she's being funny.

The kids are reasonably gentle. When any similar lapse used to happen with my mates, they'd look at me like I was the village idiot – 'Are you stupid or something?' Now at least they do actually accept there's something wrong – 'OK,' they say, 'but you're still stupid!'

With newer friends, it can feel a little more awkward and embarrassing. We had neighbours round and while they were there I asked Seren to fetch something.

'Er . . . er . . .'

She knew I'd forgotten her name. 'Come on, say it!'

'Er . . . you . . .'

'No, that's not it – what is it?'

Friends obviously know what I'm like but it still makes you wonder what people think when they see something like that.

While losing my thread used to happen once in a blue moon, now it's a daily occurrence. I find myself staggering through sentences, no certainty I'll get to the end. I want to talk but my mind is either on a break or can't process the function. The easiest option a lot of the time is to stay quiet. I won't talk to anyone because I know it's going to be hard work and I'll get annoyed with myself. But sometimes even my own silence isn't in my control. Recently I've felt there's been a bit of Tourette's slipping into how I behave. I've noticed that around the house I'll say inappropriate stuff or swear out loud. Forget everyone else, it shocks me – and I'm the one who's doing it. These outbursts make me start questioning myself. Did I do that on purpose? Was I thinking about something that made me react in that way? Am I actually just playing on the dementia? Constant self-questioning – why am I behaving like I am?

Thankfully, despite everything, Steph and I are able to have a laugh about the intruder in our lives.

She'll give me a reminder that it's bin day – 'I can't do that,' I'll tell her.

'Why not?'

'Brain damage.'

'Get lost.'

'No really – I can't remember how to get out the back gate.'

Other times, I'll tell her she's the one with the problem. While she can remember any words to any song – hence her nickname of 'The Jukebox' – try to get her to remember everything from the shops and you haven't got a cat in hell's chance. I've told her – 'Sing the shopping list and you might remember it!'

She gives as good as she gets. If she gets confused, she'll say to me, 'I've caught it off you – I'm stupid now as well.'

It's great that we take the piss out of each other – exactly how I want it. The alternative, that we sit there wallowing in the situation, doesn't bear thinking about.

Occasionally, though, I can't avoid it. It's a pointless question, because there is no answer, but I can't help asking myself, *What has she done to deserve this?* This kindest of women, this loveliest of mothers, this most giving of partners – *Why? Why her?* I wouldn't wish what she's facing on anybody. I know she'll deal with it, because she's stronger than anyone I've ever met. I'm talking real strength. Not fifteen blokes on a rugby field. Steph has incredible resilience – she's had to, being married to me. But why should she have to carry this burden? It changes nothing to say it, but I'll say it anyway – it's so, so unfair. I get it easy. I won't be able to see what's happening through the clouds of dementia. Her view will be crystal clear. The cruelty of dementia might look like it's destined for the victim; in fact it's for those left behind.

Sometimes I feel like I'm learning as much about myself as I forget. I've always enjoyed cooking but now it's taken on a greater significance as something in which I can really lose myself. I love nothing more than doing the Sunday roast, making my own gravy from scratch, preparing all the trimmings. No wonder then that I find it particularly upsetting if a memory lapse interrupts that mental escape. A few times I've been stood there, making meals I've prepared a hundred times, and completely forgotten what I'm meant to be doing. I was making a pie last week and just stopped dead. I had no idea what to do next. Steph had to help me. I was saying to her, 'I haven't got the faintest idea what goes in it.'

Reading used to be another big mental refresh. I'm trying my best to stick with it, but it's not easy when I can't remember any of what I read the last time round. I'm on the fourth in a series of detective novels at the moment, so really should be aware of the recurring characters, but still they pop up in the pages as a complete mystery to me. Reading isn't really the same when you have to keep checking back on who everyone is. What was once an escape from frustration has now become the source of it.

Retaining written information is difficult full-stop. That's hard when you're dealing with work responsibilities and, as I have just done, going through the process of buying a house. At times, people have thought I'm dyslexic. I'm not, but the fact they thought I might be is an indicator of how damage to the brain can be misinterpreted.

Alcohol I've yet to give up. Being a big lad, I've always been able to hold my drink, although nowadays I never have more than a few beers because that's not who I am any more. I have noticed, however, that even on just a couple of drinks I can get blackouts. I'll wake up the next morning and look at Steph. She knows from the expression on my face what I'm thinking – *Shit! What have I done?* She can see the panic in my eyes.

'It's all right,' she'll say, 'nothing happened. You're fine.'

'I didn't run up and down the street naked?'

'Not this time.'

The chances of public misbehaviour are mercifully slim. We'll have a few drinks with a big dinner and then a night in front of the telly with a box set – which of course I can't remember either. I never used to drink at home – for me, it was something you did when you were out – but now I'd much rather just have a couple of beers, find that little happy buzz, and have a dance round the kitchen with the kids. I don't want anything more than that. The last thing I want to do is mess up my daily routine, which involves a very early start. It has to – when you've got four small children, how else can you possibly fit in the responsibility you have to family, work and, in my case, fighting dementia?

Because I find it hard to concentrate, every little thing takes longer than it should. The frustration of making lifestyle changes to ensure I remain as fit and healthy as possible comes from time pressure. Keeping my mental state balanced means more time in front of the red lights. The nature of my job means working nights. Raising awareness of brain injury in sport means doing documentaries and interviews. Seeking financial security means dealing with legal issues.

I'm not operating in a little bubble of my own. I have people who depend on me. I was down in Portsmouth for work recently when Steph rang. Saskia had a ridiculously high temperature, Steph had been up all night with her, and now Saxon didn't seem well either. I got on the motorway straight back, bursting through the front door to find an exhausted Steph bleary-eyed on the sofa with the school run yet to do. That's family life. Millions of people juggle their commitments every day. I'm just not sure how many balls I can juggle before I start dropping one. When someone's flipped over your hourglass and the sand is running out, everything feels like a pressure.

On an average day I'll get up before six, feed the dog, and have a little time to myself before the kids come avalanching downstairs. I'll make their breakfast, do the school run – walking and scootering (I don't remember any kids being dropped off at school by car when I was a kid) – and unleash any new stockpile of mental fuzz by heading off with my fishing rod for an hour. I'll get back home, do some fitness training, catch up on some paperwork, and then the kids come home and it's back to the usual mayhem. That's it, that's my day. Well, maybe. If I'm working nights on the water, I'll be heading off with a crew in the van, not seeing my bed until five in the morning.

Thankfully, Steph doesn't work so she takes a lot of pressure off me in terms of caring for the kids. She knows, for instance, that my brain is crazily sensitive to high-pitched noises. If one of the kids squeals it's like someone has got a hot iron and slammed it down on a nerve. It's like a reflex action – I have no choice but to shout out. And then I see the kids looking at me and feel terrible. I always tell them I'm sorry. I never want my condition to upset them. Again, I'm lucky to have someone as understanding as Steph. She can tell straight away if I'm in a bad way and need to be left alone. I'm hugely appreciative of that – I'm well aware that I'm leaving her to deal with four children. It's one of the reasons why, when I'm back on the level, I try to do as much as I can with them. It's important to me that I spend every minute I can with the kids. Everyone is a ticking time bomb to some degree – no one knows how long they'll live – but for me I feel the pressure of creating the memories that will hopefully stick with them when I've turned into a completely different person. And yet the reality – the stark punch-in-the-face reality – is I have to earn as much money as I can as quickly as I can. It makes me feel desolate sometimes to see that oh-so precious family time being eaten away. I so desperately want to be there for the cuddles, the bedtimes, because I want to hardwire those memories, for them and for me. If I do end up a shell of who I was, I want them to know their dad loved them more than anything in the world. I want them to remember how it felt to be hugged by him, to be kissed by him, to feel his bristles rubbing against their face. For my part, I want to do all I can to program them into my brain, brand their names into its very core. I want to make it so the disease has to do its very, very worst before I forget.

This balancing act – money, family, self-care – is so hard. Every day I'm on a high wire in a force-ten gale trying to reach the other end. But there is another, more positive way of looking at it. My illness has brought us, as a family, closer together than I could ever have imagined. I think when they're older the children will respect us for being as open as we felt possible with them from the start, not that hiding dementia is possible anyway. They can see the evidence with their own eyes. It sounds awful because they're so young, but they have already started to read me – 'Let's leave him alone a little bit – he's not in a good way.' You have to respect kids' intelligence. It doesn't work to hide things away from them; to leave them with questions in their head.

I got upset the other day. I realised I'd forgotten the children's births, not their birthdays (which I can keep in my phone diary) but their actual arrivals in this world. This despite me being alongside Steph for all four. Each should be imprinted on my brain, but no, the eraser of dementia has rubbed them all away. The same has happened with our wedding. The basic fact that it happened in Las Vegas will, I hope, be hard to forget, but ask me about the details – the day itself, the venue, what was said – and already I haven't a clue. Like every other photo album in my house, the contents are as big a revelation to me as they would be to a stranger.

I wonder sometimes if these gaps are appearing because I'm panicking, trying too hard. You know how sometimes if you look at something straight on you can't see it, but if you look out of the corner of your eye it's there? Or maybe some kind of hidden image pops up on your phone and only right at the last, when you give up searching, does it become clear? It's like that. I want to remember stuff so badly that I fear I'm forcing my mind, and it's pushing back, playing tricks on me, hiding memories behind a curtain. Either that or it slips into panic mode – *I NEED TO REMEMBER! I NEED TO REMEMBER!* Its core function is disappearing and all it can do is shout at itself. I don't blame it – I do exactly the same. Together, the brain and I can't even put such a decline down to events slipping further and further into the past. If someone said to me, 'What did you do last week?' there'd be dark holes where entire days should be. I know some people will say they can't remember what they did yesterday, or find themselves at the top of the stairs and have no idea what they've gone up for, but this is different. There's a vacuum where many of my most treasured memories – new, old and in between – used to be. Bit by bit they are disappearing. Not forgotten. No echo to come reverberating back. Gone. Eventually I'll have a past life that exists mainly behind a wall – a wall too tall for me ever to see the beauty on the other side. The realisation of such huge emotional loss hits me with the force of the hardest tackle. The death of a memory is a concussion in itself, a deep blow to my morale, a blunt reminder of what dementia is doing to me and of what it will further strip me of.

◈

I'm really happy with where I am now with Steph and the kids. That happiness, though, is constantly being punctured by the sharp stab of inevitability. There will come a point where I can do nothing. When, instead of lifting the weight off my family, mentally if not physically, I'll be heaping that weight on them. It's one of the reasons we settled in Cheshire. I have no family support network whereas Steph's family is close by. She comes from a background totally different to me. For her, family is everything, a bond that can never be broken. If I should take a turn for the worse and Steph requires emotional help, we know her family will be absolute rocks. For them, it's natural to hold one another up. In the years before we came back to the UK, I'd been looking to the ex-pat community for that element of support. When you see how a proper family works, you understand it just doesn't compare.

We are also lucky enough to live on the edge of some beautiful countryside. What I particularly love about being back in England are the seasons. Living in the heat I'd missed seeing the landscape around me change – different colours, different shades, one day never quite being like the one before. I loved seeing the kids getting used to it, too. A couple of days after we returned, we were driving down a country road.

'Stop the car!' Seren shouted from the back.

'What? Why? What's happening?' I slowed to a halt.

'It's a sheep! It's a sheep!'

If she'd seen a camel, she wouldn't have blinked. Lions or tigers too, come to think of it. She'd seen them all at Dubai Zoo. But a sheep? It was like something from another planet.

Now she's getting used to another common sight – the camera crews that pop up at home to record my dementia fight. I think actually she quite likes it. They were filming the school run a few weeks ago. Other children were asking who the cameras were for. 'They're for us!' she said proudly, giving it a bit of swagger.

I've always played down my sporting achievements around the kids. They've never seen me play and it's not like I sit down every night and stick on videos of myself. Sometimes, though, Seren will hear a friend's parent mention something.

'Are you famous?' she'll ask me.

'No, no,' I'll say.

But I think she's twigged now that there's something about me that some people find interesting.

It's funny, when we set up home round her way, Steph was adamant that no one would have an idea who I was. 'It's all football up here,' she said. 'No one's bothered about rugby.'

It was just before Christmas and so we went into Liverpool to do some shopping. We headed to a market stall to get some wrapping paper. I was just about to pay when the bloke refused point blank. 'No, Steve,' he said, 'you have that on me for all you've done.' I gave Steph a look. She was gobsmacked.

We then met Steph's parents for lunch in a pub in the city centre. I was about to pay the bill when I noticed the drinks hadn't been included. I pointed it out because the last thing I wanted was for anyone to get in trouble. The manager came over. 'No worries, Steve,' he said, 'all the drinks are on the house. It's a treat for us to have you in here.'

I turned to Steph. 'I thought you said no one round here would have a clue who I was.' She didn't say anything – she was too busy leaning on the table with her head in her hands.

I love us all being here in our new home, happy, hunkering down, us six, our family. I've bought and sold properties in the past but this means more to me than any other. This house has been hard-earned in tough times. It hasn't come from being paid to play rugby; it's come from graft and our determination not to be beaten by an illness. To me, despite my condition, this home signifies a new start, and for that reason all we brought with us from the old one is the couches. I had no attachment to a lot of things because

I didn't remember where they came from or why I bought them, and so in a skip they went.

I wish I could throw the dementia in there as well. The other morning, I put my head in my pillow and cried. All I could think was I'd wasted my life. I'd put myself in this position, my family in this position. People keep telling me, 'It must be incredible playing for your country.' And yes, it is. But it's not worth being like this for.

'I'd give everything to do what you've done,' they say. And I think, *Go on then, go and give your life with your family* – because that's what I've done. Rugby was the making of me – it took me to amazing places, gave me incredible experiences, and introduced me to some remarkable people. But at the same time it destroyed me.

What was the point of any of it? I won seventy-three caps for England. I couldn't be prouder of that. But I can't flesh it out beyond a statistic because I don't remember so much of it.

I finally dragged myself off the mattress and went on the Peleton for half an hour. I had so much pent-up energy inside – sadness, anger, whatever you want to call it – that I came third out of 7,500 people on the session. I absolutely smashed it, and on this occasion it made me feel better. I'd emptied not the body, but the mind. Isn't that strange? Someone with dementia willingly emptying their brain? Sometimes, though, blankness is a release. I wipe the whiteboard clean. On that bright pristine surface I then draw all that really matters to me. Five amazing faces. I went back to my bed and fell soundly asleep.

Epilogue

THE DARKNESS AND
THE LIGHT

In writing this book I have tried to rebuild my mind. The foundations might be made of sawdust and the bricks made of sand but, for a while at least, I can see who I was and what I was about.

I'll be honest. There's a big part of me that's still in denial. Part of me which thinks this is all just bullshit; that it's just a big mistake and if I leave it long enough it will go away. Let's face it, I've broken my neck before now and still been fine. There's always been a way. I've always pulled something out the bag, always survived. This will be the same. Won't it?

Once I even asked John, the neuropsychiatrist, 'Is my brain just playing tricks on me? Is there actually nothing wrong?' I mean, how mad is that? Let's face it, getting my hopes up like that is only setting myself up for a fall. Convince myself

I'm absolutely fine and then suddenly something will happen – I'll forget a friend's name – and I'll be back down to earth with a thud. Other times I'll be having a chat with someone, feeling on top of the world, and suddenly realise that not a word of what they've said has gone in. I did exactly that just the other day with Steph's dad, listening but somehow not listening at the same time. The worst is if the other person forgets where they were in the conversation – 'Where was I?' they ask.

'You're asking me? You do know what's happening to me, don't you? I don't know where I was, let alone you!'

I think actually the thing that confirms I have CTE more than any other is I can never remember what those three letters mean. There is, bluntly speaking, no hope. But I'd hate anyone to think this is a book screaming 'Woe is me!' I haven't written it because I want people to look at me with a sympathetic expression; I've written it because I want to throw back the curtain on sport's not-so-little secret. I've also written it because I can see how powerful it is for the dementia message to come from someone who is living with it; someone who is themselves on that constant journey of self-discovery. I want my message to be heard, to help as many people as possible not end up in the same position.

I also want, for the sake of generations to come, everyone to comprehend how widespread brain damage, and the risk of dementia, is in sport. There have been those lobbying about the issue for years only to find, if you'll excuse the expression, they've been banging their heads against a brick wall. Yes, the knowledge of what's going to happen to me is a torture, but I take some comfort knowing that my diagnosis is helping to cast light on the invisible thousands – not just in sport but across society as a whole – trapped within dementia's clutches. We can't go on treating those who forget as the forgotten.

I expect most people who write their story hope it will be relevant for many years. I'm different. I hope one day *Unforgettable* will be seen as a historical record of the bad old days; a time when sport lost its way, became mired in tunnel vision, and put profit above responsibility. Sadly, however, change always seems to come slowly, and traumatic brain injury in sport, and its aftermath, is likely to persist in one form or another for decades.

I'm sure there are all sorts of people out there who have played rugby at all levels and are scared of the problems they may now be facing. Maybe they are in denial. Maybe they've slammed the door on the idea that their brain could be home to this alien presence. As such, I hope *Unforgettable* can act as a beacon of hope, a gentle nudge that life does go on even with dementia; that the damage it inflicts is gradual and there are, despite the lack of a coordinated national response to the dementia crisis, remarkable people and organisations out there to help not only you but those around you – those you fear for the most.

In my own heart, I need this book because what else have I got? Photos, videos of the past become meaningless. I'm in them, yet not in them. Like I was pointing a camera at myself only to discover there was never any film in it. My life – or rather my brain's version of my life – will be in my head. That's why, when dementia does finally overtake me, I ask of it one thing – to trap me not in a world of rugby, or my childhood, but to allow me to live in a space that is forever this moment – my wife Steph and our four beautiful children as I see them here in front of me now, laughing, playing, and, for the sake of realism, bickering a little as well. Give me that and on the outside I might look blank, but on the inside I will be living the happiest possible life. The picture paused at the point of perfection. Steph, Seren, Slone, Saskia and Saxon – I will be in your lives every minute of every hour. Think back to those times and you will be in mine too.

ACKNOWLEDGEMENTS

It's been weird to find out about myself through other people's memories. I can't write an autobiography – I don't know enough about the details of my own life – and so by necessity I've had to fill those gaps with the evidence of others' eyes. There have been times when people have been so kind with their recollections that I've asked myself how much I actually believe. Are they sugar-coating the real me? That's not paranoia. Truth is, not a huge number of rugby people, players or otherwise, have messaged me since my dementia was made public. That surprised me a little as I'd always thought I was good at looking after people when they had problems. Maybe I got that one wrong. I had a chat with Hephs.

'Look, tell me the truth,' I told him. 'Was I a bit of an

arsehole when I was younger? Because people aren't exactly queuing up to reach out to me now.'

He was typically straight with his reply. 'Yeah, at times you were difficult, let's put it that way.'

That took me aback a bit – I wish I'd never asked! But you can't have it all ways. I've always appreciated people who talk straight, which is why I value so much the contributions of those who have been kind enough to contribute to this book.

Among them are several players from England's World Cup-winning squad of 2003. Massive thanks to the lunatic Lewis Moody for still making me laugh, the oh-so-good-looking Ben Cohen, Joe Worsley, and the rock that is my Northampton buddy and mentor, Paul Grayson. On the coaching side, battling to make me as good as I could be, I thank Simon Hardy for his immense knowledge and patience in turning me into a decent lineout thrower (I apologise once more for the shit coffee). Andy Robinson – I couldn't respect you more. Thank you so much for the time you put into making me an England international and the way you did it, with good humour and discipline. Sir Clive Woodward, you are right – you were definitely conducting an orchestra. It's the only one I'm ever likely to be in and 'thank you' doesn't quite seem enough for spotting my place in it.

I'd also like to thank Colin Deans, a giant of the game who mentored me as a hooker at Northampton; John Steele, another massive influence; and Phil Keith-Roach for totally understanding me. Wayne Smith – if I was world class, then you were the one who made me that player.

ACKNOWLEDGEMENTS

There are plenty who steered me along the way who never saw the limelight and, I expect, would never for a single moment seek a place in it. They include the coaches who saw me through my 'rough diamond' early days. Thanks to Mark Lee, Matt Bridge and Alan Hughes. A huge and heartfelt thank you also to Keith Picton who absolutely sculpted my rugby career. Words can barely express what you meant to me.

I would like to thank Hephs, who is like family to me, for being there so often. I look up to you in so many ways. Thanks also to Andy Blay, a great friend who allows me to feel so comfortable in my own skin, and Jon Drown for being a constant steadying presence in my life. Mike McGeever – you have been a lifeline – someone I wish had been there when I was younger. Thanks also to your incredible wife, Caroline. A big mention also to Steve and Helen Wall, beautiful people and godparents to our children, and my old friend Mikey Davies in Dubai. Richard Higson and Stuart Stammers – thanks for the fun and the laughs. Shaun, Simon, Gary and Declan at SP Environmental, cheers for making the day job so enjoyable.

Ben Thomas, my agent, you have been immense, a friend and a tower of strength in difficult times. From my heart – thanks.

Thank you to all at the Concussion Legacy Foundation for your incredible awareness-raising work (to discuss brain donation email UK@concussionfoundation.org).

I would also like to thank those in the media who have

been proactive in talking about rugby's issues, telling players' stories and becoming the kind of independent truth-tellers who can make a difference.

A big thank you to James Hodgkinson, Matthew Phillips and and all at Bonnier for making this project work and being so committed, helpful and understanding from the word go. It's been a pleasure.

To my literary agent, James Wills, of Watson, Little: thank you for helping me navigate the daunting waters of starting a book and finding the right publisher for my story.

Finally, I would like to thank John Woodhouse, who worked with me on this book, for making what could have been so difficult so comfortable. I would never have written this book if you hadn't made me feel so at ease. We bonded over a bad fish-finger sandwich, became mates, and took it from there.

There will, I know, be those I have forgotten, and to them I can only apologise. Believe me when I say you are there, I'm sure, somewhere in my head.

More than anything I would like to thank my incredible wife Steph and my four beautiful children, Seren, Slone, Saskia and Saxon. You are my rocks. You are my everything. I love you more than words could ever say.

INDEX

INDEX